Living Your Legacy

An Action-Packed Guide for the Later Years

Dale Larsen
Sandy Larsen

16pt

Copyright Page from the Original Book

InterVarsity Press
P.O. Box 1400, Downers Grove, IL 60515-1426
World Wide Web: www.ivpress.com
E-mail: email@ivpress.com

©2012 by Dale and Sandy Larsen

All rights reserved. No part of this book may be reproduced in any form without written permission from InterVarsity Press.

InterVarsity Press® is the book-publishing division of InterVarsity Christian Fellowship/USA®, a movement of students and faculty active on campus at hundreds of universities, colleges and schools of nursing in the United States of America, and a member movement of the International Fellowship of Evangelical Students. For information about local and regional activities, write Public Relations Dept., InterVarsity Christian Fellowship/USA, 6400 Schroeder Rd., P.O. Box 7895, Madison, WI 53707-7895, or visit the IVCF website at <www.intervarsity.org>.

All Scripture quotations, unless otherwise indicated, are taken from the THE HOLY BIBLE, NEW INTERNATIONAL VERSION®, *NIV® Copyright © 1973, 1978, 1984, 2011 by Biblica, Inc.™ Used by permission. All rights reserved worldwide.*

While all stories in this book are true, some names and identifying information in this book have been changed to protect the privacy of the individuals involved.

Interior design: Beth Hagenberg
Cover design: Cindy Kiple
Images: Martin Barraud/Getty Images

ISBN 978-0-8308-2113-6

Printed in the United States of America ∞

 InterVarsity Press is committed to protecting the environment and to the responsible use of natural resources. As a member of Green Press Initiative we use recycled paper whenever possible. To learn more about the Green Press Initiative, visit <www.greenpressinitiative.org>.

Library of Congress Cataloging-in-Publication Data

Larsen, Dale.
  Living your legacy: an action-packed guide for the later years: 13
sessions for individuals or groups / Dale and Sandy Larsen.
       p. cm.
   Includes bibliographical references.
   ISBN 978-0-8308-2113-6 (pbk.: alk. paper)
   1. Older people—Religious life—Textbooks. 2. Aging—Religious
aspects—Christianity—Textbooks. 3. Bible—Criticism,
interpretation, etc.—Textbooks. I. Larsen, Sandy. II. Title.
   BV4580.L37 2012
   248.8'5—dc23
                                                                    2012009660

| P | 24 | 23 | 22 | 21 | 20 | 19 | 18 | 17 | 16 | 15 | 14 | 13 | 12 | 11 | 10 | 9 | 8 | 7 | 6 | 5 | 4 | 3 | 2 | 1 |
| Y | 33 | 32 | 31 | 30 | 29 | 28 | 27 | 26 | 25 | 24 | 23 | 22 | 21 | 20 | 19 | 18 | 17 | 16 | 15 | 14 | 13 | 12 |

TABLE OF CONTENTS

Introduction	ii
1: Cast Off Security	1
2: Engage with the Unexpected	12
3: Revive an Old Dream	23
4: Rescue the Helpless	37
5: Build Something New	49
6: Comfort the Downcast	62
7: Empower the Poor	74
8: Find an Alternative	85
9: Make a Connection	97
10: Notice the Children Around You	108
11: Take the Lead	119
12: Welcome the Stranger	130
13: Look to the Future	144
Conclusion	157
Appendix	168
Notes	176
Back Cover Material	185

In memory of K. Dean Wallace He lived his legacy; now his legacy lives on.

Introduction

When InterVarsity Press approached us to write a study guide about "the later years," we said yes right away.

We knew there was a need for such a book. Whether by choice or by circumstances beyond their control, people of retirement age are facing radical life changes. Former roles defined by work and family are gone or at least significantly reduced. People ask life-shaking questions: Who am I now? How should I invest these years? Must I redefine myself, and if so, how? We hope that this book will encourage people of retirement age to stay actively involved in service and invested in the lives of others, and promote confidence that in this time of transition, God still has plans and purposes for our future.

With our deadline over a year away, we spent several months putting off work for this project. Eventually we had to face up to the reason for our procrastination: we were wrestling with the very issues that the book was supposed to address. We were just as stuck as our book's potential readers. How could we write for other people if we hadn't resolved the issues ourselves?

In our case the life transition sneaked up on us and caught us unprepared. We recently moved to a new city. Through other moves we have always found our identities in various roles in community and church, but this time things are different. For the first time we are looked on as an "older couple." Physically we no longer fit the roles we once played in community theater productions. In church we are no longer tapped to lead the youth group or teach teen Sunday school. When we take advantage of senior deals in restaurants, we find ourselves in an alien atmosphere surrounded by old people.

Meanwhile our writing deadline loomed closer. We began to work on this study guide while still mired in the struggle to find our place. Not having the answers ourselves, we set out to find out what other people have done and what people in the Bible did in similar circumstances.

Through Internet searches we discovered older people in history who have launched remarkable new endeavors. Contemporary people came to light too. News clips about an elderly physician who serves at disaster scenes or a fired advertising writer who finds job satisfaction in a coffee house—once only mildly interesting items, these stories captured our attention. Most of the people we write about, however, we found closer to home, by reading the local newspaper, asking around at church and taking time to notice and listen. We met baby boomers who go on yearly international mission trips. At a conference we just happened to sit next to an older woman whom God has plunged into a new ministry of divorce care. We watched retirees hand out free food at a church and tutor immigrants in English.

Over the months, as we have worked on this guide, God has shown us some answers. Some came through our study and prayer over what to write. Others came through trial and error, going down various possible avenues of service; some ideas didn't work out, but a few did. Others were dropped into our laps, such as a volunteer opportunity which opened up while we were pursuing something else.

We wound up writing this book mostly for ourselves. Along the way it turned into a book for everyone else who shares our uncertainties and our longing to stay future-oriented. If you wonder whether God still has valuable work for you to do, and if you desire to stay in active service for the Lord and for people but aren't sure how, then this book is written for you as well as for us.

HOW TO USE THIS GUIDE

This study guide can be used by both groups and individuals. Here are the components of each session and how individuals and groups can best use them:

• **Personal Narrative.** This is a story of an individual's or group's experience. Some of the narratives are about exploring a new direction in life; others are about finding a place within an existing avenue of service. The intent is to reassure us that we are not alone in our search for purpose. At the end of each Personal

Narrative, a series of questions helps you identify with the story.

Group members should consider the questions on their own and then be prepared to discuss them with the group; individuals should answer the questions for themselves.

• **Connecting with a Bible Character.** This biblical account, told in story form, prepares you for the Bible study to follow. It helps you focus on the heart of what is going on in the biblical passage, and it leads naturally from the Personal Narrative into the Bible Study. As you read, mentally put yourself in the setting and imagine what it was like to be there.

If you are studying in a group, take time to read through this material before your meeting as you may not have time to read it within the study session.

• **Bible Study.** Here is the focal point of each session. Each study provides a biblical perspective for how to invest ourselves and our God-given abilities as we age. Each study includes questions designed to help you apply the Scripture passage to your own situation.

If desired, group members could read the Scripture passage and answer the questions in advance in order to be prepared to discuss them with the group and to listen and learn from the other group members. Or if you prefer, you can simply do the study together during the group session. Individuals should read the Scripture and answer the questions on their own, and may wish to talk over their responses with someone else.

• **Exploring Possibilities.** Here the session leaves the theoretical and dives into the solidly practical. This section urges you to examine the reasons why you make decisions, good or bad. It prods you to open yourself to new alternatives.

This section assumes individual responses. If you are studying in a group and have answered these questions in advance, you may still want to return to them at the end of the study session or later, on your own. Your time together may have brought forth new ideas.

• **Praying into the Future.** This is an opportunity to explore ideas which you see fitting into your own future. It is also a healthy time to voice apprehensions to God.

Groups may wish to pray specifically for one another and commit one another's concerns to God. You may even identify opportunities you can take on as a group or ways to join forces with a larger effort. Individuals may wish to enlist others' prayers regarding concerns that emerge.

May this book help all of us at a transitional point of life to walk into the retirement years with full confidence in God, who isn't through with us yet.

1

I

Cast Off Security

Hebrews 11:1-3, 8-12

PERSONAL NARRATIVE

Move on? At this stage of our lives? It was absurd to even consider the idea.

We were in the most comfortable situation ever. In many ways it was close to ideal. We owned our cozy and attractive home, free and clear. The large overgrown yard offered opportunities to putter around with landscaping but did not demand meticulous care. We are not big shoppers, so it was no hardship that major shopping was forty miles away. Our self-employment income for writing and self-publishing had increased dramatically while our expenses had gone down. For the first time in more than thirty years of marriage we had a substantial amount of money in the bank. We were healthy. People assumed we would retire in that town—or that we already *had* retired there. It would have been very easy to stay there forever.

And yet, neither of us felt completely at peace where we were. Our nonworking time and energy were caught up in improving the house and yard and generally making life more comfortable. Self-absorption was taking over. At the same time we missed befriending international university students and producing original theater, two things with which we had been deeply involved in other places. As the years passed, we knew we needed to make a clear-cut decision whether to stay in that town or move on. Otherwise inertia would make the decision for us.

We set a time, the coming fall, by which we would decide whether to stay or go. We prayed for God's clear guidance. We did not invite many people's opinions, because who's going to tell you to leave town? Fall arrived, and both of us were convinced it was time to leave.

But leave for where? And what guarantee did we have that "there" would really be better than "here"?

- In what ways can you relate to the feelings described above (in the past or present)? Consider not only where you live but what you are doing.

    [Space left intentionally blank in the original book]

- In what areas of your life do you deal well with uncertainty?

    [Space left intentionally blank in the original book]

- In what areas does uncertainty worry you?

[Space left intentionally blank in the original book]

CONNECTING WITH A BIBLE CHARACTER

Abram leans back on a cushion in the door of his expansive goat-hair tent. He squints at the red, setting sun and sighs deeply.

Life is good here in Paddan-Aram. His father Terah had made a wise move years ago when he picked up and took the family from Ur, journeying northwest up the well-traveled trade route along the valley of the Euphrates River. At the time there had been talk of going further, but the patriarch had decided to settle here in the vicinity of Haran.

> *"Long ago your forefathers, including Terah the father of Abraham and Nahor, lived beyond the River and worshiped other gods"* (Josh 24:2).

Now Terah is gone, and Abram is the head of the family holdings. At age seventy-five he has every reason to settle down and enjoy his inheritance. He has an abundance of servants, flocks of sheep and goats, herds of cattle. He wishes that he and Sarai had an heir, but it's too late for children now. Other than that sadness, he looks forward to a comfortable old age full of prosperity and honor.

But what's this? A strange message. From ... God. From *God?*

The gods Abram knows most about are the moon god and his consort. A message from a god could be favorable or not. It could be a promise of prosperity if you will only perform these particular rituals. It could be a warning that your life is about to go bad because you haven't worshiped in the right way.

This message from this god—no, from *God*—is different. It is a shocker. It's a command—not to perform a certain rite, but to get up and leave: "Leave your country, your people and your father's household" (Gen 12:1).

Leave? Leave his country? Leave Haran where he and Sarai are so comfortable and secure? Leave his people and his father's household? In Abram's culture people rarely did that. It would mean cutting himself off, not only from his inheritance, but from his identity.

If God is telling him to go, he will at least consider going. But go where?

"Go to the land I will show you" (Gen 12:1).

Now this is almost too much. God is going to show Abram the destination, but not until he gets there!

From Haran there are only the two likely routes to travel. One is back along the Euphrates River toward Ur; the other is south along the trade route to Canaan. Abram can either go back where he came from or go on to an unseen country. Going back doesn't fit what God is saying. "Go to the land I will show you" sounds like moving forward into the unknown. God seems to be saying, *Abram, don't go backward; don't retreat into memories. Move forward into the unknown.*

God has more to say. There is a litany of promises. Abram will become a great nation, his name will be great, he will be blessed and he will become a blessing—even to the extent of all peoples on earth (Gen 12:2-3). To an aging man married to an aging woman, with no children at all, these promises sound absurd. In any case they depend on obeying that disturbing pair of commands: "Leave ... and go."

> *"By leaving his father's household, Abram was thus giving up his inheritance and his right to family property.... When Abram gave up his place in his father's household, he forfeited his security. He was putting his survival, his identity, his future and his security in the hands of the Lord."*

Sure, Abram thinks, *if Sarai and I were thirty years younger. But now? When my wife is sixty-five and I'm seventy-five?*

> *"Since the northern and central deserts of Arabia were so inhospitable, trade routes*

> skirted them to the north, traveling up the Tigris and Euphrates river valleys, west to Palmyra and Damascus, and then south along either the coastal highway through Palestine or down the King's Highway in Transjordan."

BIBLE STUDY

Read Hebrews 11:1-3, 8-12. Background: Genesis 11:27–12:20.

Years after his initial call, God changed Abram's name to Abraham (Gen 17:5). The writer of Hebrews uses the name Abraham, by which the patriarch is known.

[1]Now faith is confidence in what we hope for and assurance about what we do not see. [2]This is what the ancients were commended for.

[3]By faith we understand that the universe was formed at God's command, so that what is seen was not made out of what was visible. (Heb 11:1-3)

[8]By faith Abraham, when called to go to a place he would later receive as his inheritance, obeyed and went, even though he did not know where he was going. [9]By faith he made his home in the promised land like a stranger in a foreign country; he lived in tents, as did Isaac and Jacob, who

were heirs with him of the same promise. [10]For he was looking forward to the city with foundations, whose architect and builder is God. [11]And by faith even Sarah, who was past childbearing age, was enabled to bear children because she considered him faithful who had made the promise. [12]And so from this one man, and he as good as dead, came descendants as numerous as the stars in the sky and as countless as the sand on the seashore. (Heb 11:8-12)

1. Consider the definition of *faith* in verse 1. In your own words, what does this mean?

    [Space left intentionally blank in the original book]

2. How do you think Abraham would have related to verse 1?

    [Space left intentionally blank in the original book]

3. What are your certainties at this point in your life?

    [Space left intentionally blank in the original book]

4. What are your hopes right now?

    [Space left intentionally blank in the original book]

5. The ancients were commended for their faith (v. 2). Why is faith in God a commendable personal quality?

[Space left intentionally blank in the original book]

6. Consider the choices that Abraham faced. Right now how does your situation reflect similar choices?

[Space left intentionally blank in the original book]

7. Considering how little Abraham knew about his future (v. 8), how can you account for his decision to obey God's call?

[Space left intentionally blank in the original book]

8. Read Genesis 12:1-4. As far as you can tell, at the time of his call, what did Abraham know about God?

[Space left intentionally blank in the original book]

9. What were some marks of Abraham's life in the Promised Land (vv. 9-10)?

[Space left intentionally blank in the original book]

10. How did Abraham's courage to venture out with God also affect his family (v. 9)?

[Space left intentionally blank in the original book]

11. How did God work miraculously in Abraham and Sarah's lives to fulfill his purposes (vv. 11-12)?

[Space left intentionally blank in the original book]

12. What did Abraham gain through his faith in God (vv. 8-12)?

[Space left intentionally blank in the original book]

13. Abraham was seventy-five when God said "I still have something for you. The greatest part of your life is yet to come." How do you respond to the possibility that God still has important things for you to do?

[Space left intentionally blank in the original book]

14. What would it take for you to make a change in your life right now (or in the near future)?

[Space left intentionally blank in the original book]

EXPLORING POSSIBILITIES

Threats to our security raise intense emotions, but security itself can remain an abstract concept. Use the following questions to think more concretely about what security looks like for you.

- Have you recently lost or given up some form of security?
    - _____ Work
    - _____ A relationship
    - _____ A particular role in life
    - _____ Standard of living

_____ Home
_____ Something else: _____
- Do you now have, but are afraid of losing, some form of security?
  _____ Work
  _____ A relationship
  _____ A particular role in life
  _____ Standard of living
  _____ Home
  _____ Something else: _____

After you have considered the above questions, pick one or more of the following further reflection questions.

- What comes to your mind when you think of *security*? Write or draw what *security* says to you. Or find an object or photograph which represents *security*.

  [Space left intentionally blank in the original book]

- In the past ten years or more, how have your certainties and hopes changed? Ten years ago, what would you have written or drawn or placed before you to represent *security*?

  [Space left intentionally blank in the original book]

- Imagine that you are Abraham receiving the message of Genesis 12:1-3 from the Lord. What questions go through your mind?

  [Space left intentionally blank in the original book]

Which of these questions relate to your current concerns, and how might you begin to process those questions?

[Space left intentionally blank in the original book]

PRAYING INTO THE FUTURE

Pray for the gift of faith and for the right attitude toward security. Pray also for guidance and for hope as you explore God's possibilities for your future.

2

Engage with the Unexpected

Acts 16:6-15

PERSONAL NARRATIVE

Equipped with a new backpacking tent, we set off in our canoe from the landing at Weaver, Minnesota, to spend a night on an island in a Mississippi River backwater. For over an hour we paddled against a strong headwind. The downwind side of the island was blocked by dense weeds and lily pads, so we had to struggle around to the windward side in order to set up camp.

Overnight the wind switched directions 180 degrees. On the mile paddle back to the landing, we would be heading straight into it. Should we leave in the afternoon as planned, or wait another day and hope the wind died? Our supplies of food and fresh water were low, and nobody knew we were out there.

There was another option. If we canoed across the wind, not very safe in a loaded canoe, we could reach the mouth of a small river where there was another canoe landing. One of us could stay with the canoe while the other walked back along Highway 61 to Weaver to fetch our car.

In late afternoon we loaded up the canoe and headed across the wind toward the river mouth. It seemed simple, but it didn't work. We couldn't find the mouth of the river. Our map showed it coming out at the end of a point of land. For an exhausting hour we slogged back and forth along the weedy shore while the sun sank lower.

At last we gave up and headed back to Weaver, not only against the wind but through masses of heavy shoreline vegetation. We were tired, hungry, discouraged and sore. As if our ordeal needed a final complication, the landing at Weaver is invisible from the water. Squinting in the low rays of the sun, we managed to recognize some trees and make our way into the channel leading to the parking lot, where ours was the sole car waiting.

This experience in the canoe seemed to us like a reflection of the rest of our lives. After several years in Illinois we had obeyed the pull of the snow and moved back up north to Minnesota, settling in Rochester because much about the city appeals to us. Thanks to a number of happy circumstances, our house is already paid off. We have some income from royalties, Social Security and private tutoring. But even with less concern for financial needs, we find ourselves at loose ends.

We selected Rochester with three areas of interest in mind: (1) We enjoy befriending international students, and Rochester is home to a branch of the University of Minnesota. (2) Several community theaters are active here, and we enjoy acting. (3) Sandy was also looking forward to teaching junior high Sunday school. At every church we've attended for several decades, all she has had to do is offer, and she has the job.

None of these things has worked out.

Rochester's University of Minnesota is just barely under way. We offered to tutor immigrants in English at a multicultural center, but most of the time no one showed up. Theater opportunities have been few. We have joined a church we love, but for the first time ever, there is no opening to teach junior high students.

Life at this point resembles our attempts to get back from that island in the Mississippi River. The direct route has failed. Now we are ranging up and down the weedy shore, trying to find the river mouth which is not where it's supposed to be.

- What are some dead-end channels you have explored recently?

    [Space left intentionally blank in the original book]

- Where did you *think* they would lead, and where did they *actually* lead?

    [Space left intentionally blank in the original book]
- What are you longing to do now, that you feel may not be possible at this point in your life?

    [Space left intentionally blank in the original book]

CONNECTING WITH A BIBLE CHARACTER

Blocked and frustrated at every turn! What's Paul thinking? What do his travel companions Silas and Timothy think?

Paul the apostle and his new preaching partner Silas left Antioch and traveled overland into modern Turkey. In the town of Lystra they took on a third partner, Timothy. So far their trip has fulfilled its purpose as "the churches were strengthened in the faith and grew daily in numbers" (Acts 16:5).

The three would naturally continue toward the west, but the Holy Spirit has prevented them from preaching the word in Asia (the western end of modern Turkey—Acts 16:6). Prevented them from preaching! It's all so strange, but they cooperate with the Spirit and turn aside into Phrygia and Galatia. Heading north, they try to go into Bithynia on the Black Sea, but the Spirit of Jesus says "no" there too (Acts 16:7). Frustration again! They continue walking along the coast of the Sea of Marmara to Troas.

> *"Two hundred miles on foot takes two or three weeks at the very least; what did the little company think they were doing, and where did they suppose they were going? This must have been something of a testing time for all of them.... It's one thing to trust God's guidance when it's actually quite obvious what to do next. It's something else entirely when you seem to be going on and on up a blind alley."*

In their rented lodging Paul sleeps uneasily that night, and he dreams. That's not unusual, but this time in his dream he sees something he never expected. It's a Macedonian—Paul can tell by his clothing—a man from northern Greece, who holds out his hands to Paul and pleads, "Come over to Macedonia and help us."

Paul is wide awake. Greece! Across the Aegean Sea into new territory! He can't wait to wake up Timothy and Silas. They've got to find a boat and get under way!

BIBLE STUDY

Read Acts 16:6-15. For a little background about the journey described in this passage, look in your Bible or a Bible atlas for a map called

"Paul's second missionary journey" or a similar title.

[6]Paul and his companions traveled throughout the region of Phrygia and Galatia, having been kept by the Holy Spirit from preaching the word in the province of Asia. [7]When they came to the border of Mysia, they tried to enter Bithynia, but the Spirit of Jesus would not allow them to. [8]So they passed by Mysia and went down to Troas. [9]During the night Paul had a vision of a man of Macedonia standing and begging him, "Come over to Macedonia and help us." [10]After Paul had seen the vision, we got ready at once to leave for Macedonia, concluding that God had called us to preach the gospel to them. [11]From Troas we put out to sea and sailed straight for Samothrace, and the next day we went on to Neapolis. [12]From there we traveled to Philippi, a Roman colony and the leading city of that district of Macedonia. And we stayed there several days.

[13]On the Sabbath we went outside the city gate to the river, where we expected to find a place of prayer. We sat down and began to speak to the women who had gathered there. [14]One of those listening was a woman from the city of Thyatira named Lydia, a dealer in purple cloth. She was a worshiper of God. The Lord opened her heart to respond to Paul's

message. [15]When she and the members of her household were baptized, she invited us to her home. "If you consider me a believer in the Lord," she said, "come and stay at my house." And she persuaded us. (Acts 16:6-15)

> "**The unique phrase** the Spirit of Jesus [v.7] may imply a vision of the Lord. On the other hand, Paul was travelling with Silas, a man known as a prophet (15:32), and the directions may have come through him."

> "For whatever reason and in unspecified ways, the Spirit at times hinders people from doing what they intended to do or from going where they planned to go. The Spirit then turns them in quite different directions, giving them undreamed of work to accomplish."

1. These short verses cover a lot of territory. Describe the stages of the journey taken by Paul, Silas and Timothy. What might they have been thinking at each stage of their journey?
   [Space left intentionally blank in the original book]
2. Suppose you meet Paul at the border of Mysia just as he realizes they are not going

to be allowed to enter Bithynia (v. 7). He tells you about their wanderings in the past few weeks. What could you say to encourage him?

[Space left intentionally blank in the original book]

3. We are not told how the Holy Spirit blocked the missionaries from entering certain areas, but apparently they were confident it was the Spirit's leading. When and how has the Holy Spirit held you back when you attempted to go into new areas of service? How did you react to the Spirit's restraint?

[Space left intentionally blank in the original book]

4. Look again at Acts 16:9-12. The word *we* in verse 10 indicates that Luke, the author of Acts, has joined the group. What compels the missionaries to go in a new direction? What would it have been like to experience and respond to this vision after the previous difficulties they have faced?

[Space left intentionally blank in the original book]

5. *Reread Acts 16:13-15.* Paul's habit in Gentile areas is to go to the Jewish synagogue (Acts 13:14, 42-44; 14:1). The missionaries go looking for the synagogue in Philippi

("place of prayer" was the term used by non-Palestinian Jews for a synagogue). Instead of finding at least ten Jewish men, the minimum required for a synagogue, they find instead a group of Gentile women. How did the missionaries respond to the unexpected circumstances they encountered?

[Space left intentionally blank in the original book]

6. After encountering yet another unexpected situation on their journey, the missionaries could have become discouraged and turned away upon meeting the group of women. How would the missionaries' experiences since leaving Antioch encourage them to do what they did: sit down and begin to speak to the women by the river (v. 13)?

[Space left intentionally blank in the original book]

7. After so many dramatic encounters in other cities, the first steps of the mission to Philippi must have appeared small. How did these first undramatic steps bear fruit right away (vv. 14-15)?

[Space left intentionally blank in the original book]

8. What difference did it make to Lydia that the missionaries chose to speak to the women on the riverbank?

[Space left intentionally blank in the original book]

9. We often overlook avenues of service because we feel they are beneath us, or because we're unsure of what engaging in them might require. What service options might you have previously overlooked that you could give new consideration? Consider possibilities in your community and in your church.

[Space left intentionally blank in the original book]

EXPLORING POSSIBILITIES

After we returned from our canoe trip, we looked up a satellite image of the river we couldn't find. It revealed that our map was wrong. The river has changed course. It no longer empties into the Mississippi from a point of land, but far back in a bay where we did not even bother to search. As with our journey, Paul and his fellow missionaries encountered several unexpected turns in their journey.

Let the options below help you explore some of the aspects of your life that may offer new opportunities for service and growth.

- Draw a riverbank. Your drawing can be anything as simple or elaborate as you like—from a few abstract lines to a full representation in watercolor or colored pencil. On the riverbank draw or write "insignificant" opportunities as the Lord shows them to you this week.

[Space left intentionally blank in the original book]

- The Holy Spirit led the missionaries to a few women outside Philippi. The mission to Philippi would not end there, but on that first Sabbath they didn't know that. Look over the "insignificant" opportunities you drew or wrote onto your riverbank sketch. Choose one. Let your imagination wander forward. Write a brief account of where that opportunity, under God's supervision, might lead you and others.

[Space left intentionally blank in the original book]

PRAYING INTO THE FUTURE

Today and throughout this week, ask the Holy Spirit to open your eyes to the needs right in front of you. Pray for the willingness to get involved.

Gerald Hawthorne writes, "Sometimes the Spirit speaks through disappointing circumstances that cause people in whom he lives to take a different but better course of action than that originally planned." Pray that the Spirit will show you those different but better courses of action.

3

Revive an Old Dream

Exodus 3:1-22

PERSONAL NARRATIVE

Five days after they were married in 1962, Dick and Sibyl Towner went to work at a private girls' camp in northwest Wisconsin. Sibyl served as head counselor and Dick served as a trip counselor, taking youngsters on wilderness trips. Love of the beauty of God's creation and the opportunity to impact college-age counselors and the campers in life-changing ways endeared them to camping. They even envisioned that they might someday own and direct their own camp, a seemingly far-fetched dream.

As Dick pursued a career in higher education administration, Sibyl continued to return to the camp with their growing family for the next sixteen summers. In 1976 Dick felt called to accept the invitation to join the staff of their church in Cincinnati as executive pastor. Shortly afterward, the church asked Sibyl to use her camping experience to establish a camping ministry at the church, which led to her eventually serving as minister to families with children and director of summer ministries (more camping!).

In 1990 Dick spent time looking deeply at what was most important to him and became a full-time church consultant for the next two-and-a-half years. In 1992 he was asked to join the staff of Willow Creek Church in suburban Chicago to develop a ministry to help people steward their resources in God-honoring ways. Sibyl's gifts became readily apparent at Willow Creek, and she served in a number of staff positions and was asked to develop a father/daughter camp ministry at Willow's camp in northern Michigan.

Through the years Sibyl and Dick continued their love of camp ministry and deepened their appreciation of the life-change that can occur when individuals are removed from their normal environments and placed where they can experience God in new and deeper ways.

As they entered their seventies, they both sensed what Sibyl calls *restlessness*, "like we were baby birds being pushed out of the nest."

They decided to move back to Cincinnati where one son and his family live, which brought them closer to other family. Someone suggested, "Why don't you think about a place with a little cabin and lake near Cincinnati?" Well, who wouldn't be attracted to that idea? One friend talked to another friend, and the thread soon led to a man who was thinking about purchasing a 150-acre retreat center, complete with lake and retreat cabins. His vision was to have a few Christian families live onsite in homes they would build and own. The Towners liked the idea that they could have their own place and blend into an existing ministry.

However, discussion and prayer soon led from just building a small cabin to a decision to enter into full partnership as co-owners/directors of the retreat center. As preparations were being made for the closing, the potential partner suddenly withdrew. Dick's first thought was that the Lord had just saved them from financial disaster! Still, both Dick and Sibyl were disappointed. Was what had seemed to be the fulfillment of that long-ago thought that maybe someday they would direct a camp-related ministry not going to happen after all?

At that point the Towners, who were now seventy and seventy-three, seemed to have two options. They could move to inner-city Chicago to be involved with a ministry they had been supportive of over the years, or they could continue pursuing the purchase of the retreat center.

Sibyl asked Dick, "What does it feel like when you think of working in the inner city?"

Dick replied, "It feels like duty and obligation."

Then she asked him, "What does it feel like when you think of the retreat center?"

He replied, "Joy!"

Sibyl agreed with the latter response. That did it. The Towners decided to pursue the purchase of King's Ranch, as the center was known. However, they knew they needed partners. *What if we asked Skip and Linda Holmes to join with us?* they wondered, thinking of a couple in Cincinnati who were very dear friends. A phone call revealed that Linda and Skip were on their way to spend six months in Bangkok, Thailand, on an assignment by Skip's employer! That development could have put an end to the dream, but the Holmes replied, "A retreat center has been a dream of ours too! We'll pray about it and call you back." A week later via a Skype call from Bangkok, the Holmes replied in the affirmative. They gave Dick power of attorney to proceed with the purchase of King's Ranch, now renamed The Springs. Sibyl says, "We now have an expanded place to help people of all ages encounter God, listen to their stories and believe that they will return to their family, work and ministry in more authentic ways."

Looking back at how the dream of owning and operating a "camp" has come to fruition, Sibyl adds, "Finding this retreat center (and most of the other significant decisions in our lives) was not the result of strategic planning. We didn't try to figure it all out. The only 'strategic plan' in it was responding to our sense of restlessness as a nudge from God to be open to what was coming our way."

- What old dreams have you abandoned? Why did you abandon them?

  [Space left intentionally blank in the original book]
- How might you look at your old dreams differently now? Are there any that might be revived, even possibly in a different way than you thought previously?

  [Space left intentionally blank in the original book]
- Are there projects you have started which have never been finished? Is this perhaps a good time to complete something?

  [Space left intentionally blank in the original book]

CONNECTING WITH A BIBLE CHARACTER

Moses did not know he was capable of murder.

He knew he was capable of study and learning. He was fluent in several languages. He was trained to fight in warfare. His royal Egyptian education put a high value on eloquence, and he was aware of his failings in that area. He knew he had been raised as the son of Pharaoh's daughter, grandson of the great Pharaoh.

On this bright morning Moses stands at the edge of a building construction site, marveling at the engineering feats of the Egyptians. He feels a heady superiority at his place in the royal household of such a nation.

Abruptly Moses turns and strides away. He knows something else about himself, something his Hebrew nursemaid told him long ago—that she was his real mother, that he is a Hebrew, a member of the enslaved foreigners expending their lives in forced labor for Pharaoh. Moses knows he belongs in those lines of people pulling those immense stones into place. If his parents hadn't hidden him along the Nile's riverbank, if his sister Miriam hadn't hung around and watched, if Pharaoh's daughter hadn't come along to bathe in the river...

You should do something about it, Moses, he thinks to himself. The people of God should not be in slavery, especially not to worshipers of the beastly so-called gods of Egypt. Perhaps it's time to act.

Alarming sounds come from around the corner of a building. Moses hears cries and sharp blows as he comes around the corner and sees an Egyptian overlord viciously beating a Hebrew slave.

Now. Now is the time. Moses takes a quick look around. He sees no one but the Hebrew slave, and he is sure to be grateful. Moses has not forgotten his military training. He steps up behind the Egyptian, pins his arms behind him and puts a muscular arm around his neck. In seconds it is all over.

The stunned Hebrew slave looks Moses in the face with full recognition, then turns and runs. *What?* Moses thinks as he sees the slave flee. *No word of thanks for his deliverer?* And now what? The body of the dead Egyptian won't be easy to explain. Moses is glad for the easy-yielding sand in which to hide the evidence of his impulsive act.

The next morning Moses has almost absolved himself of murder in his newfound zeal to rescue his people. He goes out to mingle with the Hebrew slaves and sees two of them fighting. When Moses intervenes, the aggressor pushes him aside and demands, "Who made you a ruler and judge over us? Do you want to kill me as you killed the Egyptian?" (Ex 2:14).

The word is out. Moses is a killer. And, more quickly than Moses believed was possible, Pharaoh has heard and now wants him dead.

Moses, the would-be deliverer of his people, runs for his life, fleeing east into the barren Sinai Peninsula.

BIBLE STUDY

Read Exodus 3:1-22. Background: Read Exodus 2:11-25; Acts 7:23-29; Hebrews 11:23-28.

[1]Now Moses was tending the flock of Jethro his father-in-law, the priest of Midian, and he led the flock to the far side of the wilderness and came to Horeb, the mountain of God. [2]There the angel of the

LORD appeared to him in flames of fire from within a bush. Moses saw that though the bush was on fire it did not burn up. [3]So Moses thought, "I will go over and see this strange sight—why the bush does not burn up."

[4]When the LORD saw that he had gone over to look, God called to him from within the bush, "Moses! Moses!"

And Moses said, "Here I am."

[5]"Do not come any closer," God said. "Take off your sandals, for the place where you are standing is holy ground." [6]Then he said, "I am the God of your father, the God of Abraham, the God of Isaac and the God of Jacob." At this, Moses hid his face, because he was afraid to look at God.

[7]The Lord said, "I have indeed seen the misery of my people in Egypt. I have heard them crying out because of their slave drivers, and I am concerned about their suffering. [8]So I have come down to rescue them from the hand of the Egyptians and to bring them up out of that land into a good and spacious land, a land flowing with milk and honey—the home of the Canaanites, Hittites, Amorites, Perizzites, Hivites and Jebusites. [9]And now the cry of the Israelites has reached me, and I have seen the way the Egyptians are oppressing them. [10]So now, go. I am sending you to

Pharaoh to bring my people the Israelites out of Egypt."

[11] But Moses said to God, "Who am I that I should go to Pharaoh and bring the Israelites out of Egypt?"

[12] And God said, "I will be with you. And this will be the sign to you that it is I who have sent you: When you have brought the people out of Egypt, you will worship God on this mountain."

[13] Moses said to God, "Suppose I go to the Israelites and say to them, 'The God of your fathers has sent me to you,' and they ask me, 'What is his name?' Then what shall I tell them?"

[14] God said to Moses, "I AM WHO I AM. This is what you are to say to the Israelites: 'I AM has sent me to you.'"

[15] God also said to Moses, "Say to the Israelites, 'The LORD, the God of your fathers—the God of Abraham, the God of Isaac and the God of Jacob—has sent me to you.'

"This is my name forever,
the name you shall call me
from generation to generation.

[16] "Go, assemble the elders of Israel and say to them, 'The LORD, the God of your fathers—the God of Abraham, Isaac and Jacob—appeared to me and said: I have

watched over you and have seen what has been done to you in Egypt. [17]And I have promised to bring you up out of your misery in Egypt into the land of the Canaanites, Hittites, Amorites, Perizzites, Hivites and Jebusites—a land flowing with milk and honey.'

[18]"The elders of Israel will listen to you. Then you and the elders are to go to the king of Egypt and say to him, 'The LORD, the God of the Hebrews, has met with us. Let us take a three-day journey into the wilderness to offer sacrifices to the LORD our God.' [19]But I know that the king of Egypt will not let you go unless a mighty hand compels him. [20]So I will stretch out my hand and strike the Egyptians with all the wonders that I will perform among them. After that, he will let you go.

[21]"And I will make the Egyptians favorably disposed toward this people, so that when you leave you will not go empty-handed. [22]Every woman is to ask her neighbor and any woman living in her house for articles of silver and gold and for clothing, which you will put on your sons and daughters. And so you will plunder the Egyptians."

1. Hebrews 11:23-28 implies that Moses had already made up his mind about his loyalty to the Lord, even before his encounter at

the burning bush. What words or phrases do you find in Exodus 3:1-22 which indicate that Moses already knew the Lord?

[Space left intentionally blank in the original book]

2. What emotions might Moses be feeling as he hears God's words in verses 7-10, especially considering his actions in Egypt prior to his flight to Midian?

[Space left intentionally blank in the original book]

3. Consider verses 11-12 and Moses' previous attempt to help his people in Exodus 2:11-14. What contrasts do you see in Moses' attitude?

[Space left intentionally blank in the original book]

What contrasts do you see in God's involvement in the situation?

[Space left intentionally blank in the original book]

4. How does the Lord both reassure and equip Moses in verses 13-15?

[Space left intentionally blank in the original book]

5. When have you attempted to do something, but found your efforts to be fruitless? How have you seen God at work in those times?

[Space left intentionally blank in the original book]

6. From verse 16 to the end of the chapter, God takes over the conversation. He does not tell Moses everything, but he reveals some of what will happen. How does the Lord walk Moses through at least the first part of what he is being called to do?

[Space left intentionally blank in the original book]

In what ways have you seen God walking you through difficult situations, as he helped Moses through this process?

[Space left intentionally blank in the original book]

7. How is God honest with Moses about the obstacles to come (vv. 18-20)?

[Space left intentionally blank in the original book]

8. In verses 16-22 what promises of God would give Moses confidence?

[Space left intentionally blank in the original book]

In what things have you needed confidence? How have you seen God work in those situations?

[Space left intentionally blank in the original book]

9. Review Exodus 2:23-25. What was taking place back in Egypt during Moses' self-imposed exile in Sinai?

10. How did these events in Egypt help prepare the way for Moses' return?

[Space left intentionally blank in the original book]

11. Events from our past, our sins and mistakes, may make pursuing new endeavors seem impossible, like closed doors. It can also seem, as we get older, that what once looked like possibilities begin to look more like closed doors. Which doors would you like to reopen (or open for the first time) if possible?

[Space left intentionally blank in the original book]

EXPLORING POSSIBILITIES

- Sometimes it can seem like the possibilities of our youth are locked behind closed doors. Draw or visualize a scene in which one of those doors is closed, and then draw or visualize a scene in which it is open. Or close and then open a real door in your home. Identify a dream or possibility on the other side of that door. What would keep you from going through that door if God opened it?

[Space left intentionally blank in the original book]

- Find a picture, souvenir or some other object that represents a dream you used to have for your life, one you did not follow. Make notes about how it stirs up your thoughts. What possibilities come to mind as you consider the object you have chosen?

  [Space left intentionally blank in the original book]

- Are there aspects of your old dream which you would like to revive? Sketch out or list a few possible ways you might begin to make that happen.

  [Space left intentionally blank in the original book]

- Do you know someone who has successfully revived a dream of his or her own? Make plans to contact that person and learn about how they were able to do so.

  [Space left intentionally blank in the original book]

PRAYING INTO THE FUTURE

While not every old dream deserves to be revived, God may be calling you to go back and take up a purpose to which you were once devoted but which has been lost. Pray about those doors you would like to reopen. Ask God to keep firmly closed any doors that should not be reopened, and to open doors as he chooses.

4

Rescue the Helpless

Luke 10:25-37

PERSONAL NARRATIVE

"God decided this baby needed a grandpa."

From the difference in their ages, the "grandpa" might be more like a great-great-grandpa. The baby is six-day-old Michael. The grandpa is seventy-eight-year-old Dr. Basil Jackson of Milwaukee, Wisconsin.

The unlikely setting is a tent which serves as the medical trauma center on the airfield at Port-au-Prince, Haiti. Michael was born and then fell on his head during an aftershock of the devastating Haitian earthquake of January 2010. The 7.0-magnitude quake killed hundreds of thousands of people, injured hundreds of thousands more, and made an estimated one million people homeless.

Through Hope International Ministries, Dr. Jackson arrived in Haiti with a team of physicians and others to help some of the most critically injured people. The scene was overwhelming. Dr. Dennis Hill of Hope International Ministries describes it:

The medical staff worked among two large tents, one containing the operating room and about 60 beds, the other supporting about 125 beds with a makeshift x-ray area and open-air surgical bed for conscious procedures. The latter unit contained room for about 50 children; adults filled the rest. Everyone lent both hands to every task—doctors carrying bed pans, nurses changing sheets. There was no hierarchy of privilege or status found among those who were working side-by-side from all over the world. The cumulative effect of thousands, even millions of ordinary acts, is an extraordinary effort only an all-knowing God could orchestrate.

Among his other medical skills, Dr. Jackson is a pediatric psychiatrist. His knowledge and compassion are needed in this place of suffering where many of the wounds go beyond the physical. Some of the Haitian earthquake victims are so traumatized that they cannot speak and can barely respond to anyone.

Dr. Jackson moves among the victims with compassion and wisdom. His presence is aided by the fact that he is fluent in several languages. Dr. Hill of Hope International says, "Basil is glue when things need to be put together."

Volunteering at the scene of the Haitian earthquake is nothing new for Dr. Jackson. He has volunteered at scenes of natural disaster all over the world.

Why does he do it? He explains, "I'm an old man with a deep faith, but faith doesn't count unless you do something about it in your behavior and in your actions." Clearly he takes seriously the words of James 2:17: "Faith by itself, if it is not accompanied by action, is dead."

Dr. Jackson gives enormous amounts of time and energy in the most difficult places at the most difficult times. It can never be easy or convenient for him, especially at his age.

And he plainly thrives on the giving. In the midst of the Haitian trauma center he is even able to laugh as he says, "It's just amazing, life-changing—even for an old guy who doesn't have much life left."

- Do you ever feel that you can't do much for others because you don't have enough years left?

    [Space left intentionally blank in the original book]
- For what and for whom are you willing to be inconvenienced?

    [Space left intentionally blank in the original book]

CONNECTING WITH A BIBLE CHARACTER

Jesus' disciples exchange knowing looks. Oh, no, here it comes again. An "expert in the law" has a question for Jesus. They're always coming around with questions, usually insincere questions.

Of course it's normal procedure to open a discussion with a rabbi by posing a hard question, and this one is fairly common: "What must I do to inherit eternal life?" It isn't a casual question, because eternal life is a weighty matter. This particular law expert, however, carries himself with an irritating air of self-righteousness. His attitude says, *Whatever is necessary for eternal life, I've already done it.*

Jesus does not answer the law expert directly. Instead he responds by asking him what is written in the Law, that is, the five books of Moses. The lawyer knows his stuff. His reply comes straight from the books of Deuteronomy and Leviticus: Love God and love your neighbor. Everybody knows that. Jesus agrees and commends him for a good answer.

Ah, but it's not over, as the disciples knew it would not be. The lawyer comes back with the challenge, "And who is my neighbor?" It's obvious what he thinks: not Gentiles, not Samaritans, not Jews who disregard the Law, not lowlifes, not sinners.

Now this is an interesting question. The disciples look at Jesus. How is he going to answer? What does he think the Scriptures mean by *neighbor*?

Jesus replies, "A man was going down from Jerusalem to Jericho..."

As he often does, Jesus is going to give his answer in the form of a story. It will be a story with a desolate setting. The disciples and the lawyer know all about that road from Jerusalem to Jericho. It descends with alarming steepness through rocky lonely places. All kinds of bad things can happen there. The disciples shift their weight, settle in and prepare to hear the story. The lawyer looks guardedly interested.

With breathtaking brevity, Jesus' story shifts from brutality to indifference to compassion. A man is robbed and left for dead; that's the dread of everyone who travels the hazardous Jericho road. Two potential rescuers come along, upright religious people; that would be the hope of any victim on that road.

Then the story takes a turn that makes the law expert and the disciples squirm. The "holy" people ignore the brutalized man, pull up their robes and pass by on the other side. Jesus' listeners ask themselves: *Would I do that? Would I want that done to me?*

The beaten man's situation looks hopeless. Then Jesus pulls a surprise. "But a Samaritan..." A Samaritan? One of those unclean half-Jewish, half-Gentile heretics who claim that God's temple in Jerusalem is the wrong place to worship? What's he doing in this story? Oh ... he's the hero! He goes out of his way to help the injured man. He does the good that the "good" people didn't do.

Jesus' listeners are stunned. The disciples are glad that Jesus' concluding question is aimed at the law expert and not at them. Which one proved to be a neighbor? Well, of course, the least likely one, at least from their perspective: the Samaritan.

BIBLE STUDY

Read Luke 10:25-37. For background on the conflict between the Jews and the Samaritans, read 2 Kings 17:24-41.

[25]On one occasion an expert in the law stood up to test Jesus. "Teacher," he asked, "what must I do to inherit eternal life?"

[26]"What is written in the Law?" he replied. "How do you read it?"

[27]He answered, "'Love the Lord your God with all your heart and with all your soul and with all your strength and with all your mind' and, 'Love your neighbor as yourself.'"

[28]"You have answered correctly," Jesus replied. "Do this and you will live."

[29]But he wanted to justify himself, so he asked Jesus, "And who is my neighbor?"

[30]In reply Jesus said: "A man was going down from Jerusalem to Jericho, when he was attacked by robbers. They stripped him of his clothes, beat him and went away, leaving him half dead. [31]A priest happened

to be going down the same road, and when he saw the man, he passed by on the other side. [32]So, too, a Levite, when he came to the place and saw him, passed by on the other side. [33]But a Samaritan, as he traveled, came where the man was; and when he saw him, he took pity on him. [34]He went to him and bandaged his wounds, pouring on oil and wine. Then he put the man on his own donkey, brought him to an inn and took care of him. [35]The next day he took out two denarii and gave them to the innkeeper. 'Look after him,' he said, 'and when I return, I will reimburse you for any extra expense you may have.'

[36]"Which of these three do you think was a neighbor to the man who fell into the hands of robbers?"

[37]The expert in the law replied, "The one who had mercy on him." Jesus told him, "Go and do likewise."

1. What was behind the lawyer's questioning of Jesus (vv. 25-29)?

   [Space left intentionally blank in the original book]

2. Picture the scene just after the robbery (v. 30). How would you describe the robbery victim?

   [Space left intentionally blank in the original book]

3. The priest and the Levite preserved their ritual purity, yet they sinned against the wounded man by ignoring him (vv. 31-32). How might our desire to preserve our spiritual purity keep us from seeing or being involved with people who need our help?

[Space left intentionally blank in the original book]

> *"The origins of the Samaritans are linked with the account in 2 Kings 17:24-41 about how, following their conquest of the northern kingdom, the Assyrians colonized the area by settling it with people from a number of Mesopotamian towns, including Cuthah. These colonists adopted the Israelite faith alongside their own religion (v. 41), and their descendants ... are the Samaritans of later times. The hostilities between Judah and her northern neighbor recorded in the books of Ezra and Nehemiah demonstrate the antiquity of the division between the two groups."*

4. How did the Samaritan differ from the priest and the Levite in his attitude (v. 33)?

[Space left intentionally blank in the original book]

5. How did the Samaritan differ from the priest and the Levite in his actions (vv. 34-35)?

[Space left intentionally blank in the original book]

> *"Jews and Samaritans traditionally had no love for each other; although violence was the exception rather than the rule, the literature of each betrays an attitude of hostility toward the other. Jesus' illustration would offend Jewish listeners, striking at the heart of their patriotism, which was religiously justified."*

6. To what extent was the Samaritan willing to be inconvenienced for the wounded man (vv. 33-35)?

[Space left intentionally blank in the original book]

7. What risks did the Samaritan take by stopping to help the wounded man?

[Space left intentionally blank in the original book]

8. Who are some people in your community who are robbed, beaten and stripped of what they have in one way or another and are bypassed by others?

[Space left intentionally blank in the original book]

9. What are some attitudes of religious people in your community toward the people you thought of in question 8?

[Space left intentionally blank in the original book]

10. Think of someone (an individual or a group) whom you personally would rather bypass. Why would you rather "pass by on the other side"? What might help you refrain from avoiding this individual or group?

[Space left intentionally blank in the original book]

11. The Samaritan went to considerable expense to help the wounded man (v. 35). What do you think he received in return?

[Space left intentionally blank in the original book]

12. Jesus told the lawyer, "Go and do likewise" (v. 37). In what ways do you sense the Lord leading you to follow this command?

[Space left intentionally blank in the original book]

EXPLORING POSSIBILITIES

In the autumn of 2010, heavy rains in our area of Minnesota caused floods which wiped out several very small towns. Though the event barely made a blip on the national news, for the residents of those towns it was—and still is—a Hurricane Katrina – scale disaster. Thousands of volunteers came to help with cleanup and rebuilding. A new nonprofit organization called Zumbro Valley Disaster Recovery was formed to give grants to families who had lost everything in the floods. At Christmas, three months after the disaster, volunteers welcomed a dozen flood-victim families to an American Legion Hall for a turkey dinner, a visit from Santa and gifts for all the children.

Volunteers have brought many different skills to the Zumbro Valley recovery effort. Rebuilding a house requires construction skills, but the "skills" required to save Christmas for those families included sensitivity, organization, gift buying, food preparation and playing Santa Claus.

- Consider the skills you have which could help people in crisis. Besides your professional and educational skills, include the "skills" of friendliness, familiarity with finding your way around town, extra time on your hands or extra room in your car. You probably do not possess all the skills of Dr. Basil Jackson, but you can offer support to professional helpers. The scene does not have to be a natural disaster. Think of volunteering at your local medical center's information desk where

people come in with their own personal crises going on. Consider being a mentor for a prisoner on probation, or encourage at-risk kids through a big-brother-big-sister program.
- Through local news media, bulletin boards, the Internet and word of mouth, be on the lookout for local crises that cry out for volunteer help.
- Think outward to places further away. Could you offer your hands for a week of work in a place that needs rebuilding, either building or supporting those doing the rebuilding?

PRAYING INTO THE FUTURE

Reconsider your answers to Bible Study questions 8, 9 and 10. Pray for a more compassionate attitude toward those people you thought of. Thank God for his mercy and that he did not pass you by on the road. Ask God to show you where and how to get involved with people who are in crisis.

5

Build Something New

Genesis 6:5-22

PERSONAL NARRATIVE

Sally and Ken met at a Bible institute, where as music majors they were often thrown together. On a visit home with Ken for Christmas, Sally witnessed a dispute among his family members that degenerated into adult temper tantrums. The experience should have been the first red flag in their relationship.

"We were married at age twenty-one," she recalls, "a naive, overprotected young woman and a young man from a highly dysfunctional family who lived for the praise of other people and controlled his world by anger." The second red flag should have waved as the newly married couple drove away from the church, with a "Just Married" sign on the car, and Ken whistled at a woman on the street.

The couple became music teachers at a Bible institute in France. Sally excused Ken's flirtatious behavior with other women as "part of his personality." Then female coworkers and students began to confess their involvement with Ken.

The couple both lost their jobs at the institute. The director sent them to the study center L'Abri in England for three months, but Sally felt she could not speak honestly for fear of Ken's angry reaction.

"I felt like I was dying," she says. "All that I loved had been taken away—people, ministries, even our children who were in boarding school." The couple changed missions and spent the next twenty years teaching in Europe. Ken was involved in several suspicious relationships but never with proof enough for an accusation.

Sally says "I lived in the same house with the corpse of a marriage for over twenty years." She never filed for divorce or separation because, says Sally, "I was a coward. I have always hated and avoided conflict. Although my husband never struck me, I believed he was capable of hurting me. Second, I believed no one would believe me. Third, I knew any ministry would be finished. The incomprehensible thing is that God seemed to be blessing our ministry. People were coming to the Lord."

The couple retired and returned to Canada. Two years later Ken was diagnosed with acute leukemia. Three weeks later he died. Standing at his bedside while he was in a coma, Sally realized that "I had nothing to say. He had never admitted to being unfaithful or asked for forgiveness. He died with our forty-year conflict unresolved. I was devastated. Yet his death also made me free—free to be me."

For a time Sally lived a nomadic life serving at branches of L'Abri in England, Canada and the Netherlands. During her time at L'Abri in the Netherlands, God clearly changed the direction of her life and ministry. She was seventy-one years old.

A recently divorced young woman came to help at L'Abri, and she and Sally made an immediate connection. Several weeks later an older woman arrived as a L'Abri student. She was reeling from a recent divorce from a husband of twenty-five years. Sally also received calls from two friends and former colleagues who were divorced or in the process of divorce from husbands who were professing Christians.

Sally made up a survey for divorced women in ministry. She was shocked to discover that the women felt their churches had done nothing to help them through the crisis, and that their greatest challenge was in going to church, where they felt judged, avoided and alone. Sally looked at the survey results and said, "Okay, Lord. What is going on here? What are you saying?"

Back home in Canada, God confirmed for Sally that she was to begin a ministry in Divorce Care (www.divorce care.org) to reach out with hope and healing to this "forgotten people group." A pastor in a nearby town had prayed for three years for a way to help the hurting divorced people in her parish. Sally, the pastor and another woman from her church held their first Divorce Care meeting in the café section of an old general store owned by a woman who was also a divorce survivor. Seven people were at the first meeting, and several weeks later another person joined them.

At age seventy-one, out of painful circumstances and a painful relationship, Sally has entered a new avenue of ministry which she had never imagined.

- When you are asked to do something you have never tried before, how do you react? And why?

    [Space left intentionally blank in the original book]

- What has happened in your life that could be the spark for starting something new?

    [Space left intentionally blank in the original book]

CONNECTING WITH A BIBLE CHARACTER

Just a small corner, a fragment; no, more like a grain of sand compared with the distant mountain peaks. That's how Noah thinks his own grief compares with the grief of God. God must be grieved and angry over the state of humanity. People don't even try to conceal their sins. They are constantly in open rebellion against the God who created them and who gives them the gifts of sunlight, food, families, and so many things to enjoy.

Long ago Noah set his heart to follow God, but he feels alone. Except for his immediate family, he is alone in his faith. He looks in vain for any love for God and fear of God in the people around him.

God's patience astounds Noah. Sometimes Noah is surprised that God hasn't given up on humanity and wiped them all out.

Noah senses the Lord stirring him, speaking to him as he considers the world he surveys. Even given his grief over the disobedience of humankind against the Lord, he is stunned by what the Lord tells him to do, and what will soon happen. *Lord, you are going to do what?* God has reached the end of his patience. He is going to wipe out humanity from the face of the earth. A knife of grief hits Noah to think he will share the fate of all humanity when he has tried to be faithful.

But God has not finished speaking to Noah. The destruction will come by water, and God is giving Noah instructions for building a boat. Noah's heart leaps. A boat means salvation for him and his family! It won't have to be very big, just big enough for...

Second Peter 2:5 strongly implies that Noah verbalized his reasons for building the ark. Noah is called a "preacher of righteousness." Here the Greek word for preacher means "a herald," one who gives

> *a proclamation. It is not the same as one who gives good news.*

The scope of this project is overwhelming. Noah's mood sinks. What kind of boat is this? It's gigantic! Such a thing has never been done before! He can hardly expect help from the people around him. He and his family will have to do this construction job on their own. It's the only possible escape from God's coming wrath. The ark means life for them. But this ark is so big, so unprecedented, so apparently useless, so apparently—does he dare say it?—ridiculous!

BIBLE STUDY

Read Genesis 6:5-22. For background, read all of Genesis 6–8. This is the story of God's judgment on the world and his mercy to the family of Noah, the "heir of the righteousness that is in keeping with faith" (Heb 11:7).

[5]The LORD saw how great the wickedness of the human race had become on the earth, and that every inclination of the thoughts of the human heart was only evil all the time. [6]The LORD regretted that he had made human beings on the earth, and his heart was deeply troubled. [7]So the LORD said, "I will wipe from the face of the earth the human race I have created—and with them the animals, the

birds and the creatures that move along the ground—for I regret that I have made them." [8]But Noah found favor in the eyes of the LORD.

[9]This is the account of Noah and his family.

Noah was a righteous man, blameless among the people of his time, and he walked faithfully with God. [10]Noah had three sons: Shem, Ham and Japheth.

[11]Now the earth was corrupt in God's sight and was full of violence. [12]God saw how corrupt the earth had become, for all the people on earth had corrupted their ways. [13]So God said to Noah, "I am going to put an end to all people, for the earth is filled with violence because of them. I am surely going to destroy both them and the earth. [14]So make yourself an ark of cypress wood; make rooms in it and coat it with pitch inside and out. [15]This is how you are to build it: The ark is to be three hundred cubits long, fifty cubits wide and thirty cubits high. [16]Make a roof for it, leaving below the roof an opening one cubit high all around. Put a door in the side of the ark and make lower, middle and upper decks. [17]I am going to bring floodwaters on the earth to destroy all life under the heavens, every creature that has the breath of life in it. Everything on earth will perish. [18]But I

will establish my covenant with you, and you will enter the ark—you and your sons and your wife and your sons' wives with you. [19]You are to bring into the ark two of all living creatures, male and female, to keep them alive with you. [20]Two of every kind of bird, of every kind of animal and of every kind of creature that moves along the ground will come to you to be kept alive. [21]You are to take every kind of food that is to be eaten and store it away as food for you and for them."

[22]Noah did everything just as God commanded him.

1. What was the state of humanity in Noah's time (vv. 5-7, 11-13)?

   [Space left intentionally blank in the original book]

2. How did the character of Noah contrast with the character of the people around him (vv. 8-9)?

   [Space left intentionally blank in the original book]

3. Difficult as it may be, try to put yourself in the place of Noah as God begins to speak to him in verses 13-14. How do you react to what you hear?

   [Space left intentionally blank in the original book]

> *"When all the people around him were immersing themselves in evil and earning the wrath and judgment of God, Noah set his heart to follow the path found in the person and character of God. He stood his ground and remained uninfluenced by all that was happening around him. The word* righteous *simply means that he accepted and used the righteous standard for his living and acting. It does not imply perfection."*

4. What is unusual, even outlandish, about God's instructions to Noah?

    [Space left intentionally blank in the original book]

5. Still putting yourself in the place of Noah, how do you react as you hear God's specific instructions in verses 15-21?

    [Space left intentionally blank in the original book]

6. Speaking as yourself now, what goes through your mind when you face doing a task which feels too big for you?

    [Space left intentionally blank in the original book]

7. Noah is often portrayed as the target of mockery by the people who watched him build the ark. The Scripture does not say he was mocked; nevertheless, what

comments and questions might have been aimed at Noah as he worked?

[Space left intentionally blank in the original book]

> *"The ark that Noah builds (Gen 6–8) is a huge construction, symbolic of the magnitude of the task God entrusted to the one person of virtue in this day.... The ark was approximately 450 feet long and 75 feet wide and was divided into three stories of about 15 feet each."*

8. Hebrews 11:7 says, "By faith Noah, when warned about things not yet seen, in holy fear built an ark to save his family. By his faith he condemned the world and became heir of the righteousness that is in keeping with faith." Noah stands in absolute contrast to the world around him: a righteous man in a world of sinners, building something of ridiculously immense size with no apparent purpose. What do you think kept him working?

    [Space left intentionally blank in the original book]

9. Consider this: "Noah's ark was not designed to be navigated—no rudder or sail is mentioned. Thus the fate of the company aboard was left in the hands of God." Think

of a task you took on for which you felt like you had "no rudder or sail." How did you see God guide you and provide for you?

[Space left intentionally blank in the original book]

10. What did you learn about yourself, and about God, through the experience you recalled in question 9?

[Space left intentionally blank in the original book]

What do you continue to learn through experiences such as this?

[Space left intentionally blank in the original book]

11. Recall a big job which stared you in the face—and you avoided it. What different perspective does the story of Noah give you about that job?

[Space left intentionally blank in the original book]

12. Think of an intimidating task which faces you now. How does Noah's obedience to God encourage you to face that task?

[Space left intentionally blank in the original book]

EXPLORING POSSIBILITIES

Noah's construction of the ark was not simply a useful project like adding a room onto a house. It was God's vehicle for a daring rescue from a world gone wrong. This week consider your own dissatisfaction with the way things are. Make note of all the times you think or say things like:

- Why doesn't somebody ... (for example, Why doesn't somebody clean up the trash in the Veterans Memorial Park?)
- It's not right that ... (for example, It's not right that some adults in our community can't read well enough to get a job.)
- It's about time that ... (for example, It's about time that our church reached out to the people in that apartment building just behind us.)
- More people should ... (for example, More people should give their time to volunteer in the church nursery.)
- It upsets me that ... (for example, It upsets me that we don't have an organized way to make sure our older people and disabled people always have a ride to church.)

When you have recorded a few dozen responses, look them over. What patterns do you find? Your frustrations reveal where you see holes in your world. They show the empty spaces of what you wish were being done that is not being done.

- Look at the questions you asked above. What are the empty places in the world that concern you or cause you to grieve for the world? What is one small or large thing you can do to help fill one of those empty spaces?

[Space left intentionally blank in the original book]

- It's very likely that Noah did not build alone and that his sons were cobuilders with him. Who else do you know who is interested in those gaps where things are not being done? How can you enlist that person's help?

[Space left intentionally blank in the original book]

PRAYING INTO THE FUTURE

Noah was not afraid of the ark's being too big, too unusual or even too outlandish. Or if he was afraid, he didn't let his fear stop him from building. Pray for courage as you consider new ideas for taking on the jobs that no one else is doing. Pray also for guidance, so you commit your time and resources wisely.

6

Comfort the Downcast

2 Corinthians 1:1-11

PERSONAL NARRATIVE

"That could be me. I could be without a home."

The person who said those words has a good job and can provide for his large family, but he and others in our community have come to realize that all their security could fail them, that one day they could lose everything and have nowhere to go. Their eyes have been opened by volunteering with Interfaith Hospitality Network.

Interfaith Hospitality Network (IHN) of Greater Rochester, Minnesota, is not a traditional homeless shelter where one person can show up and stay overnight. IHN serves homeless families with children age sixteen and under. Families must be referred by a social service organization such as the Salvation Army or county social services. The mission of IHN is "to help homeless families with children under the age of sixteen achieve and sustain their independence by providing them with food, shelter and a caring environment while they are in crisis." Interfaith Hospitality Network is an affiliate of the national organization Family Promise (www.familypromise.org).

Volunteers from nearly fifty local churches make IHN hospitality possible. Fifteen of the churches are rotating host sites where three to four guest families can stay for a week at a time.

Here is how it would work for a family coming into the IHN network. Two volunteer evening hosts arrive at the host church at 5:00p.m. to welcome the guest family. The hosts may be two adults or an entire family. Additional volunteers arrive to cook and serve a meal, and the evening hosts eat with the guest family. The guest family's privacy is respected. One volunteer explains, "We don't ask the families a lot of questions. They're already answering so many questions about themselves from various agencies. If they want to talk, that's okay, but we don't push them."

Later in the evening two volunteer overnight hosts arrive, and at 9:00p.m. the doors of the host church are locked. The guest family sleeps on air mattresses in their own room with linens provided. There are clear rules: no alcohol or drugs; must be in by 9:00p.m.; lights out at 10:00p.m.; and the family must work their stabilization plan.

In the morning after breakfast, the guest family goes to the Interfaith Hospitality Network

Day Center house. School-age children go to school, perhaps by bus or with a van driver.

During the day, a family stabilizer counselor works with the guest family to help them find employment and housing. The counselor networks with the family, but the family must do the work of making contacts and following through on leads. Two evenings per month the counselor sets up life skills training classes covering financial, parenting, rental and legal issues. The Day Center house serves as the family's home address and phone contact as they look for work and for a long-term place to live.

In the evening the family returns to the host church to eat and sleep. Again they are welcomed and served by the evening hosts, cooks and overnight hosts. If the family has not found housing by the next Sunday evening, they move to a different host church. Churches which are not set up to keep families overnight provide volunteers and financial support.

IHN volunteers are people of all ages, from retirees to families with young children. Because the guest families all have children under sixteen, host "grandparents" add a vital presence of steadiness and stability.

One IHN volunteer remarks that meeting the homeless families has broken down her stereotypes of homelessness. She says, "These are parents who love their children. They don't want to be in this situation. They're trying to take care of their children as best they can."

For families in the midst of the uncertainty and insecurity of being without a permanent home, senior volunteers (as well as volunteers of all ages) put a human face on the welcoming love of God.

- Think of a time when you've been in need of comfort or assistance. How did you see God's comfort during that time?

    [Space left intentionally blank in the original book]

- How have difficult experiences equipped you with new insights and skills to help people?

    [Space left intentionally blank in the original book]

CONNECTING WITH A BIBLE CHARACTER

Those Corinthians! Sometimes Paul wants to grab them and shake them. Other times he wants to put his protective arms around them. Most of the time his affection wins out. From his lodgings in Macedonia to the north, he writes them a letter in preparation for his visit to Corinth.

The Corinthian believers live in a conflicted environment of prosperity and ungodliness. To be exact, Corinth is *ungodly* only in its failure to acknowledge the one true God. Otherwise the city has plenty of gods. It is full of temples, shrines and sanctuaries dedicated to one god or another or to the Roman emperor. Most notorious is the temple of Aphrodite where temple prostitutes "aid" visitors in worship. Two centuries ago the Romans demolished the city, and for many years the site lay abandoned. Then about a century later Corinth was reestablished as a Roman colony by Julius Caesar. The site strategically controls the isthmus between the Aegean and Adriatic Seas. Thriving commerce attracts a diverse population from all over the Roman world.

Although Paul has many friends in Corinth, he also has enemies who are busy spreading negative tales about him. They say he can't be trusted. They cast doubt on his authority as an apostle of Jesus Christ. And yet Paul gave birth to the church in Corinth, where he lived and worked at making tents with Priscilla and Aquila to support himself (Acts 18). He is grieved to think that the believers could lose confidence in him and believe such slander.

The Corinthian church has already endured divisions and immorality. Not long ago Paul wrote them a sharp letter of discipline (2 Cor 2:3-4; 7:8). The issues were so painful that Paul decided to put off an earlier planned visit (2 Cor 1:23–2:1).

Now Paul's colleague Titus has arrived from Corinth with the report that the Corinthians are repentant and that their hearts yearn for Paul to visit them. With a buoyant heart Paul writes that "God, who comforts the downcast, comforted us by the coming of Titus, and not only by his coming but also by the comfort you had given him. He told us about your longing for me, your deep sorrow, your ardent concern for me, so that my joy was greater than ever" (2 Cor 7:6-7).

Paul knows that his visit may turn out to be difficult for himself and for the Corinthian Christians. Still he believes in God who comforts the downcast. He wants the Corinthians to feel abundant comfort from God, and he wants to share with them in God's comfort.

BIBLE STUDY

Read 2 Corinthians 1:1-11. Paul writes his letter not only to the Christians in the city of Corinth but to "all his holy people throughout Achaia" (v. 1). Achaia corresponds to what is now southern Greece. The fact that there were believers throughout Achaia indicates that despite their problems, Christians in Corinth had been acting as Christ's ambassadors (2 Cor 5:20).

> Paul, an apostle of Christ Jesus by the will of God, and Timothy our brother,
>
> To the church of God in Corinth, together with all his holy people throughout Achaia:
>
> [2]Grace and peace to you from God our Father and the Lord Jesus Christ.
>
> [3]Praise be to the God and Father of our Lord Jesus Christ, the Father of

compassion and the God of all comfort, [4]who comforts us in all our troubles, so that we can comfort those in any trouble with the comfort we ourselves receive from God. [5]For just as we share abundantly in the sufferings of Christ, so also our comfort abounds through Christ. [6]If we are distressed, it is for your comfort and salvation; if we are comforted, it is for your comfort, which produces in you patient endurance of the same sufferings we suffer. [7]And our hope for you is firm, because we know that just as you share in our sufferings, so also you share in our comfort.

[8]We do not want you to be uninformed, brothers and sisters, about the troubles we experienced in the province of Asia. We were under great pressure, far beyond our ability to endure, so that we despaired of life itself. [9]Indeed, we felt we had received the sentence of death. But this happened that we might not rely on ourselves but on God, who raises the dead. [10]He has delivered us from such a deadly peril, and he will deliver us again. On him we have set our hope that he will continue to deliver us, [11]as you help us by your prayers. Then many will give thanks on our behalf for the gracious favor granted us in answer to the prayers of many.

1. Consider the first lines of Paul's letter (vv. 1-7). What words or phrases would you use to describe the tone of Paul's writing?

   [Space left intentionally blank in the original book]

2. What relationship do you see here between the comfort we receive from God and the comfort we give to others (vv. 3-5)?

   [Space left intentionally blank in the original book]

3. How has "the Father of compassion and the God of all comfort" (v. 3) comforted you in difficult times?

   [Space left intentionally blank in the original book]

4. When has God used other people to comfort you?

   [Space left intentionally blank in the original book]

5. How could it be said that the sufferings of Christ overflow into the lives of Christians (v. 5)?

   [Space left intentionally blank in the original book]

6. What is the connection between Paul's suffering and the suffering of the Corinthians (vv. 6-7)?

   [Space left intentionally blank in the original book]

7. What might be some wrong motives for offering sympathy?

[Space left intentionally blank in the original book]

8. What forms of comforting show the most respect for the other person?

[Space left intentionally blank in the original book]

9. Paul briefly mentions the hardships he endured in Asia (vv. 8-9). He apparently refers to the two or three years he spent in Ephesus (Acts 19). What purpose has Paul come to see in his hardships?

[Space left intentionally blank in the original book]

10. Paul expects the Corinthians to pray for him and his associates (v. 11). How have difficult times led you more deeply into prayer?

[Space left intentionally blank in the original book]

11. When you are in difficulty, whose prayers do you ask for, and why?

[Space left intentionally blank in the original book]

12. What does Paul hope to see as an outcome of his own and the Corinthians' troubles (vv. 10-11)?

[Space left intentionally blank in the original book]

13. What purposes have you come to see in difficult times of your own?

[Space left intentionally blank in the original book]

> *Two Greek words Paul uses, both translated "comfort," are the noun paraklesis, a calling to one's side, and the corresponding verb parakaleo. Both words are closely related to parakletos, which refers to the Holy Spirit (Jn 14:16, 26; 15:26; 16:7) and to Christ himself (1 Jn 2:1).*

EXPLORING POSSIBILITIES

A friend of ours once told a story of how she and her family were comforted years ago by a small gesture of kindness. Her husband had left her with three small children. They were struggling with very little means. At Christmas two people from their church arrived with a bag of groceries and cards with money for the children. The children are now adults, but they have never forgotten and still talk about that kind gesture. Perhaps to the givers it was no big deal, but for that family it was huge.

- When you've gone through a tough time, who was an instrument of God's comfort for you? Think of several examples.

[Space left intentionally blank in the original book]
- What do you especially remember those people doing (or not doing) that helped you? Why was it helpful to you?

  [Space left intentionally blank in the original book]
- What do you especially remember those people saying (or not saying) that helped you? Why was this helpful to you?

  [Space left intentionally blank in the original book]
- What do you remember people doing or saying that was *not* helpful? Why didn't it help?

  [Space left intentionally blank in the original book]
- Who around you could use some comforting now? What are some practical ways you can offer that person comfort?

  [Space left intentionally blank in the original book]

After you've worked through the questions above, choose one or two of the action points below to follow.
- Go back to the Personal Narrative above. Have you ever ministered to people in a way similar to the program described here? Look for a similar program in your neighborhood

and learn what is involved in joining the ministry.

- Throughout the next week or month observe those around you and pray for those who are in pain or distress to receive and know the Lord's comfort. Write down your prayers.

PRAYING INTO THE FUTURE

Paul anticipated that "the prayers of many" would lead to a harvest of thanksgiving to God (2 Cor 1:10-11). Thank God for the people who have given you comfort when you needed it. Pray for the people you know who need comfort. Ask for wisdom to offer comfort that is genuine and that shows respect and concern for the other person.

7

Empower the Poor

Isaiah 58:6-12

PERSONAL NARRATIVE

International short-term mission trips have become almost routine with Western church youth groups. Today the baby boom generation is challenging the youth-group stereotype, as they have spent most of their lives challenging other stereotypes.

Jim and Suzanne Greenleaf and Kevin Schill are Minnesotans who have created what they call a service travel experience. They lead volunteer trips to Guatemala to help, empower and become friends with people of Mayan heritage. The Greenleafs go once a year; Kevin usually leads more than one trip each year.

Jim and Suzanne offer a substantial list of reasons why older people make good service travel volunteers:

- Older adults can pay their own way, while teens or college students have to do fundraising first.
- Trip leaders don't have to feel responsible for keeping track of older adults.

- Many have experienced impoverished cultures before and are aware of the needs.
- They are not looking to build a resume but are there to serve.
- They are curious about everything and really want to learn.
- As Suzanne puts it, "They're just fun!"

Older adults bring considerable life skills with them to service travel, both skills they have used in their careers and other abilities. Jim recalls, "On our last trip one doctor built a potter's wheel and taught villagers how to mold clay and fire pottery. We try not to say 'no' to any ideas people have."

Recently, twenty people from Minnesota, most of them over fifty years old, spent ten days in Guatemala to work with people in three Mayan villages in the western highlands. A five-person "dream latrine team" built latrines. Others gave informational classes on nutrition, safe water, self-esteem and family planning. Charles Butler, a Spanish-speaking eighty-two-year-old, organized day care for children while their mothers attended classes. The service group held a health fair each afternoon, which included solar oven demonstrations and dental hygiene instruction. They fit villagers with reading glasses, took blood pressure measurements and even took family photos.

Suzanne recalls, "We wrote a simple handbook for the women on nutrition and hygiene, and we had it translated into Spanish. The women who received these were so grateful. They had never had a book of their own."

One of the boomer group's goals in Guatemala was the installation of over fifty ONIL stoves. These simple, innovative stoves cook a meal with three sticks of wood and vent the smoke out of the house. ONIL stoves were developed to be compatible with traditional Mayan cooking methods, yet they are more efficient and safer than the traditional "three-stone fire," a wood fire in an open fire pit in a one-room home. The stoves are supplied by HELPS International, a nonprofit corporation which partners with individuals, businesses, corporations and local and national governments to alleviate poverty in Latin America. (For more information, see www.helpsintl.org.)

For the trip organized by the Greenleafs and Kevin Schill, donors in the United States purchased the ONIL stoves. A Guatemalan social worker chose the recipient Mayan families based on need. The families purchased the concrete blocks and venting and helped install the stoves, creating a family stake in the project.

The Greenleafs find that older volunteers like the concept of a service travel experience. They want to participate in work projects that are well prepared and organized, and then have time to travel and see other parts of the country—not only the sites pictured in travel brochures but others far off the typical tourist path.

Jim says, "People tell us how nice we are to do this for the people of Guatemala. Actually we're being selfish. We get so much out of it. This is not selfless!"

- Whom do you know who has been on a short-term mission or service trip? What was their response to the experience?

    [Space left intentionally blank in the original book]

- When have you found giving and serving to be so rewarding that it almost seemed selfish?

    [Space left intentionally blank in the original book]

CONNECTING WITH A BIBLE CHARACTER

Griping! Grumbling! Complaining! Isaiah is tired of listening to it.

If these people could just once get a glimpse of God as Isaiah did long ago in the temple, their demands would quickly shut down. They would stop whining and start thanking God for his generosity, especially his mercy. "Woe is me!" That's what Isaiah said when he saw God. God forgave his sins and commissioned him to speak to the people. To be fair, God did warn Isaiah that the people wouldn't listen (Is 6:1-13).

> **"In the Old Testament the religious use of fasting is often in connection with making a request before God. The principle is that the importance of the request causes an individual to be so concerned about his or her spiritual condition that physical necessities fade into the background."**

Now Jerusalem is threatened by attack from Assyria. The people have prayed and have fasted as part of earnest prayer, but God has not responded as they think he should and as they think they deserve.

If the people can't see God, they should at least mentally step back and look at themselves. Sure they're abstaining from food, wearing sackcloth and ashes and looking miserable. But what else are they doing? Exploiting their workers. Quarreling. Leveling accusations against each other. Talking maliciously about each other. Breaking the Sabbath.

Isaiah wants to shout, "God is not impressed with how much you abstain from eating! If you want to fast, then abstain from oppressing each other. Abstain from injustice. Abstain from doing your own business on the Sabbath. Start sharing what you have with people who have less. Do what's just and fair. Then you'll see results from God!"

BIBLE STUDY

Read Isaiah 58:6-12. The context of Isaiah 58 is the complaint of Israel. They make demands of God: "Why have we fasted, and you have not seen it? Why have we humbled ourselves, and you have not noticed?" (Is 58:3). God replies that they fast only for their own selfish motives (Is 58:3-5).

[6]Is not this the kind of fasting I have chosen:
to loose the chains of injustice
And untie the cords of the yoke,
to set the oppressed free
And break every yoke?
[7]Is it not to share your food with the hungry
and to provide the poor wanderer with shelter—
when you see the naked, to clothe them,
and not to turn away from your own flesh and blood?
[8]Then your light will break forth like the dawn,
and your healing will quickly appear;
then your righteousness will go before you,
and the glory of the LORD will be your rear guard.

[9] Then you will call, and the LORD will answer;
you will cry for help, and he will say: Here am I.

If you do away with the yoke of oppression,
with the pointing finger and malicious talk,
[10] and if you spend yourselves in behalf of the hungry
and satisfy the needs of the oppressed,
then your light will rise in the darkness,
and your night will become like the noonday.
[11] The LORD will guide you always;
he will satisfy your needs in a sun-scorched land
and will strengthen your frame.
You will be like a well-watered garden,
like a spring whose waters never fail.
[12] Your people will rebuild the ancient ruins
and will raise up the age-old foundations;
you will be called Repairer of Broken Walls,
Restorer of Streets with Dwellings.

1. Name some of the marks of the "fasting" of which God approves (vv. 6-10).

[Space left intentionally blank in the original book]

2. How could the behaviors of verses 6-10 be considered *fasting*? Fasting from what?

[Space left intentionally blank in the original book]

3. If fasting is a form of worship, then God considers the actions named in verses 6-10 as worship. How does this idea challenge your concept of worship?

[Space left intentionally blank in the original book]

4. What can you say in general about the people who are the focus of the activity in verses 6-10?

[Space left intentionally blank in the original book]

5. What does God's call for this type of active fasting tell you about the heart of God?

[Space left intentionally blank in the original book]

6. What promises does God make to people who fast in these ways (vv. 8-12)?

[Space left intentionally blank in the original book]

7. Think of people in your own community who need food, shelter and clothing, as the people mentioned in verse 7. What do you think about when you think of those people and their problems?

8. If you do not know of anyone in your community who has the needs mentioned in question 7, what can you do to expand your perspective?

9. Going beyond your own community, where are the neediest places you know about in your country?

   throughout the world?

10. Verse 12 promises that the person who lives out the fast which God requires will be called "Repairer of Broken Walls" and "Restorer of Streets with Dwellings." In what practical ways might a person today be called a Repairer of Broken Walls? Think of both physical and spiritual "walls."

11. In what practical ways might a person today be called a Restorer of Streets with Dwellings? Think of both physical and spiritual "streets."

[Space left intentionally blank in the original book]

12. Consider again the areas in questions 7 through 9. In which of those areas can you see yourself offering help, and how?

[Space left intentionally blank in the original book]

EXPLORING POSSIBILITIES

- Today we are inundated with news of disasters all over the world: earthquakes, famine, civil war, floods and other catastrophes. It's easy to become numb to all the bad news and see it from an impersonal distance. By contrast, relief organizations often highlight personal stories to illustrate their work in areas of crisis. This week, make a special effort to go to websites of relief organizations and read the personal stories they contain. Suggested websites:
    - World Relief (www.worldrelief.org)
    - World Vision (www.worldvision.org)
    - Samaritan's Purse (www.samaritanspurse.org)
    - TEAR Fund (www.tearfund.org)
    - Your own denomination's website
- After you've viewed these websites, consider which of the stories you read most moved you. What about them struck you? What

inspired you? What might you do now as a next step?

[Space left intentionally blank in the original book]

- Make an inventory of skills from your professional and personal life that you could bring to a service travel experience.

[Space left intentionally blank in the original book]

- Here are a couple of online resources to help Christians find service opportunities. Take time to explore both of them and others that you discover.
  - www.missionfinder.org/retirees.html
  - www.rvics.com (Roving Volunteers in Christ's Service)

PRAYING INTO THE FUTURE

Fasting is always difficult, whether fasting from food or fasting in the active ways of Isaiah 58:6-12. You may feel overwhelmed by the needs you see on mission websites and in your increased sensitivity to the news. You may find yourself wanting to go help everywhere, and as a consequence going nowhere. Pray for wisdom and guidance to focus your attention where you can serve best, as well as for the means to be most helpful.

8

Find an Alternative

When Retirement Isn't an Option

Genesis 21:8-21

PERSONAL NARRATIVE

Michael Gates Gill did not plan to retire at age fifty-three, but that was the age at which "retirement" was forced on him. Up until then his life had been golden. His father was a writer for *The New Yorker,* and he grew up shuttling between luxurious homes in New York City and rural Connecticut. He met legendary writers: Ernest Hemingway, T.S. Eliot, E.B. White, Robert Frost.

After graduating from Yale, Gill was practically handed an elite job as an advertising writer with a topflight New York agency. For twenty-five years he built a glittering career in a cutthroat atmosphere. He would go anywhere anytime for a client. Once on Christmas Day he left his children crying in the midst of their presents when he got a call to fly to Detroit and shoot some television commercials.

Then the advertising agency's leadership changed. The new president wanted younger people. Gill was summoned to a breakfast meeting with a younger executive whom he had championed a few years earlier. She told him he was fired. Michael Gill left the restaurant and walked down the street, weeping, with nowhere to go.

Gill pulled himself together and ran his own consulting company for ten years, but business began to fall off. Through a series of bad choices, he lost his marriage and wound up living alone in a small apartment. For the first time ever, he desperately needed a job of any kind.

Gill was nearly sixty-four when he made a nostalgic visit to a Manhattan neighborhood where he had lived as a child. He entered an upscale coffeehouse, one of the few indulgences he could still afford, and walked straight into a "hiring open house." Almost as a joke, the interviewer asked him if he wanted a job. He said yes. He was hired, not at the coffeehouse in his old neighborhood but in an area of Manhattan where he had never set foot, an old white guy among a staff of African Americans whose average age was twenty.

Now addressed by everyone as "Mike," Gill rode the subway to work, mopped floors, cleaned restrooms and washed windows. He learned to greet customers and handle the cash registers, which he dreaded. He learned the distinctions between the various coffee drinks and caught on to individual customers' preferences. He learned to take orders from a female supervisor decades younger than himself.

In his previous insulated life Gill had never known anyone like his coworkers. They were honest people with limited options in life, people who struggled to make it while their backgrounds constantly worked against them. He began to like and admire them. Gill saw how cooperation and mutual support could replace aggressive competition. He also found out that he no longer needed the things he used to buy and that he could enjoy life on his sharply reduced salary. His first Christmas at the coffeehouse, Gill realized that the store had become his new home, his coworkers his new family. Walking toward the subway one night he stopped and announced out loud, to no one in particular, that he was happier than he had ever been in his life.

> I had ... fallen, like Alice through a rabbit hole, into a great world I could never have imagined ... where people could be nicer, and the work environment better, than I had ever believed possible. Or maybe ... it was more like going through a magic door, like in *The Lion, the Witch and the Wardrobe*, and discovering some sense of wonder and surprise again.

- Michael Gill made some surprising discoveries doing work he had associated with people he once considered beneath him, in a world he knew little about. How do you respond to his story?

[Space left intentionally blank in the original book]

- To what extent is your image of yourself and your worth tied to a career or role you used to have, or which you may have to give up soon?

[Space left intentionally blank in the original book]

CONNECTING WITH A BIBLE CHARACTER

"Get rid of that slave woman and her son!"

Hagar can still hear Sarah fling the harsh demand at Abraham. Sarah didn't even use their names, *Hagar* and *Ishmael*. No, it was "that slave woman and her son." The problem was that Ishmael was also Abraham's son.

Hagar halts by a clump of withered desert bushes. Ishmael comes alongside her. He fastens his eyes on the water skin that Hagar still carries. She shakes her head. It's empty.

It's all Sarah's fault. It was all Sarah's idea. Sarah came up with a solution to the problem of being old and childless. She ordered Hagar into Abraham's tent. Hagar, only an Egyptian maidservant, had no choice but to cooperate.

The memory stings like the hot sand. When Sarah's idea worked, Sarah promptly regretted it. Hagar admits that she gloated over Sarah's barrenness. Sarah mistreated her and Hagar ran away into the desert, hardly a friendly place for a pregnant woman alone. But then the Lord called out to Hagar by name. He told her to go back to Sarah, and he gave her promises for herself and for her unborn son. "You are the God who sees me," Hagar marveled then. "I have now seen the One who sees me" (Gen 16:13).

Now Sarah has her own son, Isaac, and there is no room in the family for Ishmael and Hagar. A bag of food and a skin of water are all Abraham gave them as he sent them out into the wasteland of Beersheba.

The promises of God! What good are they now that the water is gone and the heat is beating down on an unprotected mother and her son? That other time, back then, God arrived with promises, but where is God now?

Hagar can do nothing more for her son. She wants to stay with him until the end, but she can't bear it. She leaves Ishmael in the pitiful shade of a shrub, walks away and collapses on the sand, sobbing.

And then it happens. God *is* here with them. Again, a promise comes. And water! There's a well—why didn't she see it before? Hagar hurries to fill the water skin. She carries it, dripping and fresh and cold, to her son and watches him drink. Then she quenches her own thirst. She refills the skin and pours it over both their heads while both of them laugh in the bright sun.

God *is* going to provide for them. They have a future. He is still the One who sees!

BIBLE STUDY

Read Genesis 21:8-21. For background on these events, read Genesis 16:1–18:15 and 21:1-7.

[8]The child grew and was weaned, and on the day Isaac was weaned Abraham held a great feast. [9]But Sarah saw that the son whom Hagar the Egyptian had borne to Abraham was mocking, [10]and she said to Abraham, "Get rid of that slave woman and her son, for that woman's son will never share in the inheritance with my son Isaac."

[11]The matter distressed Abraham greatly because it concerned his son. [12]But God said to him, "Do not be so distressed about the boy and your slave woman. Listen to whatever Sarah tells you, because it is through Isaac that your offspring will be reckoned. [13]I will make the son of the slave into a nation also, because he is your offspring."

[14]Early the next morning Abraham took some food and a skin of water and gave them to Hagar. He set them on her shoulders and then sent her off with the boy. She went on her way and wandered in the Desert of Beersheba.

[15]When the water in the skin was gone, she put the boy under one of the bushes. [16]Then she went off and sat down about a bowshot away, for she thought, "I cannot watch the boy die." And as she sat there, she began to sob.

[17]God heard the boy crying, and the angel of God called to Hagar from heaven and said to her, "What is the matter, Hagar? Do not be afraid; God has heard the boy crying as he lies there. [18]Lift the boy up and take him by the hand, for I will make him into a great nation."

[19]Then God opened her eyes and she saw a well of water. So she went and filled the skin with water and gave the boy a drink.

[20]God was with the boy as he grew up. He lived in the desert and became an archer. [21]While he was living in the Desert of Paran, his mother got a wife for him from Egypt.

1. The servant Hagar bore Abraham's son Ishmael. Later Abraham's wife Sarah bore Isaac, the child of God's promise. Isaac is *the child* of verse 1. How and why was Hagar banished from Abraham's household (vv. 8-13)?

[Space left intentionally blank in the original book]

2. Before Abraham sends Hagar and Ishmael away, God reassures Abraham about Ishmael's future (v. 13). It does not appear that Hagar is told of this promise. What difference does it make in your life to consider that God is working behind the scenes in ways unknown to you?

[Space left intentionally blank in the original book]

3. Imagine that you are Hagar at the moment you and Ishmael leave to go into the desert (v. 14). What do you want to say that you can't say because of your position?

[Space left intentionally blank in the original book]

4. As Hagar and Ishmael set out, what do you think Hagar expects to happen?

[Space left intentionally blank in the original book]

5. When have you felt something akin to what Hagar felt as they left?

[Space left intentionally blank in the original book]

6. What words or phrases would you use to describe Hagar and Ishmael's situation in verses 15-16?

[Space left intentionally blank in the original book]

7. Both Hagar and Ishmael are weeping (vv. 16-17). Surely they have left a good life

behind them, to face only a bleak future. As you consider how your future looks now, what causes you to grieve over what you have lost?

8. How does God intervene to provide for Hagar and Ishmael (vv. 17-19)?

9. How does God offer Hagar reassurance and hope?

10. God shows Hagar a well of water where she thought there was none. Perhaps there actually had been none (v. 19). In what areas of your life has your "skin of water" run out and things look dangerously dry?

11. When have you seen God provide for you (or for your family) when it did not seem humanly possible?

12. In the desert God said to Hagar, "Do not be afraid" (v. 17). When you think about your future prospects, where do you

especially need God to say to you, "Do not be afraid"?

[Space left intentionally blank in the original book]

EXPLORING POSSIBILITIES

A friend in his fifties recently said, "Ours is the last generation that will be able to retire." He took an early retirement and considers himself fortunate to have gotten out with a secure pension. Another friend makes a similar prediction. After he retires from his current job, he expects to have to keep working in some way in order to survive.

- If you are already retired, are you still finding it necessary to work for pay? What are your attitudes toward your new job(s)?

    [Space left intentionally blank in the original book]

- If you have not yet retired, do you anticipate still needing to work for pay? How does that prospect look to you?

    [Space left intentionally blank in the original book]

- What new opportunities for ministry might present themselves to you in a lower-wage, lower-status job? Think about contacts with people you would never have met otherwise. For example, a local Christian school has hired several older people as custodians. The school is happy to have these "grandparent" figures present for the children. What would be the blessings of that kind of job?

- What emotional barriers stand between you and a lower-wage, lower-status job?

- Make an inventory of the skills you have that other people need and would pay for. Can you repair computers? Teach guitar? Fix broken steps? Do any kind of automotive work? Cut grass? Cut hair? Trim hedges? Paint a house (interior or exterior)? Decorate cakes? Pet-sit? Organize people's closets or garages? Make Christmas wreaths? Build fences? Sew? Decide on an hourly or by-the-item rate and advertise your services everywhere you can think of. (Be sure to familiarize yourself with IRS rules for self-employment.)

- Explore the resources that are available in your community for older people to find work or job training. Following are some useful websites to help older workers find paid employment:

- www.experienceworks.org
- www.aarpworksearch.org
- www.workforce50.com
- www.retirementjobs.com
- www.careeronestop.org (sponsored by U.S. Dept. of Labor)
- www.doleta.gov/seniors (Senior Community Service Employment Program, sponsored by U.S. Dept. of Labor)

PRAYING INTO THE FUTURE

Pray for trust—trust in the Lord to open your eyes to alternatives, to provide for you, to guide you and to help you overcome reluctance to find alternative work. Acknowledge that God is still "the God who sees me" today, just as God saw and cared for Hagar and Ishmael.

9

Make a Connection

Deuteronomy 24:19-22

PERSONAL NARRATIVE

Free food? Could it be true? In our self-employment adventure, work comes and goes, and lately it had done more going than coming. Some help with groceries sounded attractive, but free food? There had to be a catch to it!

Our friend insisted there was no catch. "You can get a grocery bag full of food three times a week at Bethel Lutheran Church. It's all left over from restaurants and grocery stores and hospitals and places like that. It's perfectly good food that would otherwise get thrown away."

"How do you qualify? What's the income limit?"

"No income limit. You just provide your name and address and how many adults and children are in the household. But it's not only for families with children. It's for anybody. And you meet all kinds of interesting people standing in line!"

We did go to Community Food Response, and we did meet interesting folks in the line going down the steps to the church basement. Most of them were younger than we are. Some were parents with young children. In the church kitchen a small army of volunteers of all ages hustled back and forth between refrigerators and freezers and counters. True to our friend's word, we received a bag filled with prepared foods such as cooked meats, chili, soup, deli sandwiches and salads. Some of the food was fresh, some frozen, and all high quality.

The roots of Community Food Response go back to a snowstorm almost twenty years ago, when three hundred people failed to show up for a big event at the Mayo Civic Center. LeAnn Hanson, events coordinator for the hotel caterers, was appalled to see three hundred perfectly good dinners get thrown away.

Later LeAnn and her husband learned about a food rescue program in Kentucky. They thought how different it would have been if Rochester had a food rescue program. LeAnn suggested the idea to the other "food" people at the hotel. The head chef took the concept to the local association of chefs, caterers and restaurant owners, who liked the idea and committed themselves to "rescuing" leftover food.

Phyllis Jacobs, a CFR volunteer from the beginning, praises the group's excellent organization. Before they collected and gave out any food, they recruited an attorney, an accountant, a public health department representative, a volunteer coordinator and a representative from Mayo Civic Center event planning. The volunteer coordinator, Lois McDougall, recalls that "Bethel Lutheran Church offered rent-free space, food providers were on board, public health developed a food safety plan. We set up an accounting system, wrote articles of incorporation and bylaws and applied for nonprofit status. I developed a volunteer recruitment plan that depended on churches, businesses and schools to recruit the 15-22 volunteers needed each distribution day."

CFR provides the food donors with one-quart plastic containers. (The containers account for about 98 percent of CFR's expenses.) The donors package the food for pickup by CFR volunteers, who pack it into coolers and take it to the church. On distribution days, volunteers work in two shifts, one to organize the food and one to give it out. Excluding major holidays, food distribution is every Monday, Wednesday and Friday, 5:00-6:30p.m., year-round.

Lois McDougall emphasizes that local churches are essential to CFR's success. "All but one food distribution day each month has been adopted by a local church, and each congregation provides the 20+ volunteers needed for that day. Also a significant portion of the financial support comes through area churches."

For us the most gratifying part of going to Community Food Response was the overwhelmingly positive mood in the church. It's humbling to stand in line for any handout, but

we felt that recipients and volunteers were all in the effort together.
- What efforts like Community Food Response, which match up need with resources, exist in your area?

    [Space left intentionally blank in the original book]
- How does a program like Community Food Response give retired people an opportunity to help younger people?

    [Space left intentionally blank in the original book]

CONNECTING WITH A BIBLE CHARACTER

Naomi is back! Everyone in Bethlehem remembers the famine time when Naomi, her husband and their two sons left for the country of Moab. It was an odd destination, for Moab and Judah had a history of hostilities, but the family departed full of hope for a new start in life. Now Naomi is three times bereaved. Her husband and two sons all died in Moab. "Call me Bitter," she says, and her voice and posture reveal her wounded heart.

> *The agricultural year in Israel gave extended opportunities for gleaning. "Olives were harvested at the beginning of the*

> year—i.e., the middle of September to the middle of November, by beating the trees with long sticks (Deut. 24:20; Isa. 17:6). In March-April flax was harvested by cutting it off near the ground, then laying the stalks out to dry (Josh. 2:6). The harvesting of barley took place in April or early May, while the wheat harvest occurred in May-June. During August-September the summer fruits—figs, grapes, and pomegranates—were harvested."

Naomi does not return to Bethlehem alone. With her is Ruth, the young Moabite widow of one of the two sons. Naomi tried to persuade Ruth to stay in Moab, but Ruth insisted, "Your people will be my people and your God my God" (Ruth 1:16). Two impoverished widows, one of them a foreigner. They manage to establish a home together, but how will they support themselves?

Ruth surveys the barley fields that they passed as they approached Bethlehem. It's harvest time. Ruth has heard about the just and fair laws that God gave Israel through Moses. God instructed Israelite farmers to leave some of their grain, olives and grapes unharvested. The extra produce was for the alien, the fatherless and the widow. Between the two of them, Naomi and Ruth meet all those qualifications!

The next morning Ruth gets up early and heads out to the fields. Reapers are busy cutting the barley with sickles and binding it into sheaves. Ruth follows them. Gleaning is backbreaking work. Stoop to pick up the bearded stalks. Avoid sharp stubble. Try to keep the seed spikes from shattering. Stuff the stalks into your bag. Stoop again. Keep in mind that you still have to beat out the grain before you go home with your harvest.

The more grain Ruth picks up, the more her hope rises. *There will be enough. Naomi's God is my God and he is providing for us. Thank God for his just laws that have put together our need and the bounty of this harvest.*

BIBLE STUDY

Read Deuteronomy 24:19-22. God gave these laws to the Israelites while they were still in the desert. Long before they arrived in the promised land of Canaan and began to farm, God was already providing in advance for all the people. He built into his laws ways for the more prosperous Israelites to take care of those in hard circumstances.

> [19]When you are harvesting in your field and you overlook a sheaf, do not go back to get it. Leave it for the foreigner, the fatherless and the widow, so that the LORD your God may bless you in all the work of your hands. [20]When you beat

the olives from your trees, do not go over the branches a second time. Leave what remains for the foreigner, the fatherless and the widow. [21]When you harvest the grapes in your vineyard, do not go over the vines again. Leave what remains for the foreigner, the fatherless and the widow. [22]Remember that you were slaves in Egypt. That is why I command you to do this.

1. What are the instructions about overlooked produce (v. 19)?

    [Space left intentionally blank in the original book]

2. What are the instructions about deliberately leaving some produce unharvested (vv. 20-21)?

    [Space left intentionally blank in the original book]

3. In both of the above cases, what purpose does this law serve?

    [Space left intentionally blank in the original book]

4. Consider the three categories of people for whom the produce is to be left (vv. 19-21). What do "the foreigner, the fatherless and the widow" have in common?

    [Space left intentionally blank in the original book]

5. What is the responsibility of the gleaners (those who were allowed to take the extra produce)?

[Space left intentionally blank in the original book]

6. What is the responsibility of the landowners and reapers?

[Space left intentionally blank in the original book]

7. Nothing is said about lean years when the harvest is not bountiful. How would the promise of verse 19 encourage farmers to obey this law even in meager years?

[Space left intentionally blank in the original book]

8. God tells the farmers to "remember that you were slaves in Egypt" (v. 22). Why would leaving produce for the poor remind them of their own slavery?

[Space left intentionally blank in the original book]

9. How does gleaning preserve the dignity of the people who receive the leftover produce?

[Space left intentionally blank in the original book]

10. In what ways can you identify with the plight of "the foreigner, the fatherless and the widow"?

[Space left intentionally blank in the original book]

11. In what ways can you participate in activities or work that alleviates the suffering of those in your community who may be abandoned or forgotten?

[Space left intentionally blank in the original book]

> *"Since the bounty of the harvest is a reflection of God's covenant promise, it is only just that the owners of fields and orchards share a portion of their harvest.... Such a provision served several purposes. It insured that the entire community participated in the humanitarian efforts to sustain the poor (see Lev 23:22). The practice of leaving a portion of a field unharvested may also be tied into the regular fallowing of fields (Ex 23:10-11), which allowed the land to rest and regain its fertility. In the ancient Near East in general it is likely that what was left in the fields was originally associated with sacrificial offerings to local fertility gods. By designating this produce for the poor, rather than local deities, the biblical writer both removes the taint of false worship and establishes a practical welfare system."*

EXPLORING POSSIBILITIES

One person may have an eye for the assets in a community, while another person spots the liabilities. Efforts like Community Food Response happen when liabilities get successfully matched up with assets.

- The idea of Community Food Response arose when someone saw good food going to waste. What goes to waste in your community?

    [Space left intentionally blank in the original book]

- Community Food Response is an example of linking up needs with resources. Think about possibilities for linking up needs with resources in your own community. Consider:
    - food
    - clothing
    - child care
    - homework help
    - home repairs and maintenance
    - time
    - other resources: _____
- Create a chart matching up resources with needs in your community. You will probably have a lot of false starts and reworkings of your chart.
- Who else in your community might care about putting unused resources to use? Contact those people and talk over

possibilities for making the resources available to those who need them.

[Space left intentionally blank in the original book]

PRAYING INTO THE FUTURE

Thank God for the bounty he provides. Pray for guidance in effectively using unused resources to meet the needs of less fortunate people. Pray for others to get involved in sharing God's bounty.

10

Notice the Children Around You

Mark 9:33-37; 10:13-16

"Son, you are too young."

Twelve-year-old Jesse Overholtzer was crushed at his mother's words. He knew he was a sinner. He desperately wanted to know God's forgiveness.

The time was 1889, the place an orange grove plantation in California. The Overholtzer family belonged to a Christian fellowship with roots in the German Anabaptist movement. Jesse had gathered that being baptized and joining the church were equivalent to gaining salvation. He had never seen a person his age baptized, only adults. When he told his mother that he wanted to be baptized and join the church, her answer was gentle but firm. "You are too young." To Jesse, his mother was telling him that salvation was not for twelve-year-olds.

What does a twelve-year-old boy do when he is told that he cannot get out from under God's judgment? Jesse Overholtzer reasoned, "If I'm lost and can't get saved, then I can't get any more lost." Later he wished he could forget his years from age twelve to twenty. He left home, lived self-indulgently and wound up destitute before he came to his senses and returned to his parents. While in college he put his faith in Christ. At last his childhood longing to be baptized and join the church was fulfilled.

Overholtzer became a zealous lay preacher, but he began to lose the peace and certainty he had known in Christ. His failure to conform to the strict rules of his church made him question his own salvation. Overholtzer recalled, "I soon began doubting my salvation, for I saw that if salvation was by works, only perfect works could be accepted by God." Jesse Overholtzer married, had several children and tended a prosperous farm in California while he continued to preach, but he felt himself a prisoner of law.

A scarlet fever epidemic in 1914 quarantined the family and gave Jesse time to study the Bible all over again. He came to the conviction that salvation is by faith in Christ alone. When the quarantine was lifted, Overholtzer went back to the pulpit preaching a new gospel. As he feared, his denomination did not approve. After over a year of conflict, Overholtzer parted company with his church.

Several years later, studying the sermons of British preacher Charles Haddon Spurgeon, Overholtzer was startled to read that "a child of five, if properly instructed, can as readily believe and be regenerated as anyone." He was skeptical, recalling his own mother's words when he was twelve: "You are too young."

As an experiment of sorts, Overholtzer explained salvation to a nine-year-old boy from a non-Christian home and asked if the boy wanted to accept Christ as Savior. To his surprise, the boy did so. Later Overholtzer led a ten-year-old girl to Christ. Soon there were twenty new young converts. Overholtzer reserved judgment; the children might only have wanted to please him. But he saw that their lives were transformed.

At an evangelistic meeting, the mother of two of the girls accepted Christ herself.

She said that her reason was the changed lives of her daughters. Overholtzer heard the mother's voice as the voice of God leading him into a new ministry to children.

Overholtzer taught Bible classes and visited churches to make his case for evangelizing children. He recruited people from many denominations. He cranked out weekday Bible class lessons on a mimeograph machine and set up a training school for the teachers. There was no regular financial support. Jesse and Anna Overholtzer now had nine children and no outside jobs. They had to rely on God to provide for them and for the new ministry.

In the summer of 1933, during the Chicago World's Fair, Overholtzer went to Chicago to pioneer a training school for evangelists to children. He was fifty-six years old. Today age fifty-six does not sound old, but the man who got off the train in Chicago was approaching the life expectancy for a male in the United States in 1933. Yet his attitude was steadfastly aimed toward the future. By 1935 he was ready to initiate a nationwide effort to reach children. He had no money or supporters, but he had a genius for recruiting influential people for the cause. He made appointments with pastors of large churches and leaders of other Christian ministries, boldly enlisting them in the new movement. Their approval gave credibility to the new ministry.

The new organization was named Child Evangelism Fellowship. Today CEF ministers in 160 countries through Good News Clubs, camps and online ministries.

As one early supporter recalled of Jesse Overholtzer, "He saw so clearly the job that needed to be done, he assumed everyone else had the same vision. It never occurred to him that anyone would fail."

- What are some of your early memories of children's ministries?

    [Space left intentionally blank in the original book]
- Other than your own children, who are the children in your life who concern you the most?

    [Space left intentionally blank in the original book]

CONNECTING WITH A BIBLE CHARACTER

The disciples are relieved. Jesus has led them into new territory, south from Galilee into Judea and across the Jordan River. Maybe here he will forget those strange ideas about being betrayed to his enemies and killed. That can't be right. Jesus has only great things ahead of him. From their association with him, the disciples expect great things for themselves too.

They are still embarrassed at the memory of what happened back in Capernaum. On the way there, out of Jesus' hearing—or so they thought—they compared opinions about which one of them was closest to Jesus and which one deserved to rank highest in the coming kingdom. They had not reached a consensus when Jesus suddenly asked them what they were arguing about on the road. Of course he already knew. He made one of his usual topsy-turvy statements. If you want to be first of all, he said, you must be last of all. As an object lesson he brought in one of the children of the household.

That child at Capernaum had embodied humility. Fine. This crowd gathering around now, on the other hand, is anything but humble. The disciples and Jesus have escaped the Galilee hordes only to meet a mob of parents leading toddlers and toting babies.

You can't hear anything Jesus says over all the fussing, giggling, crying and squealing. And talk about pushy parents! They crowd forward. They tug, herd and carry their children toward Jesus. They all want him to touch their children and bless them. How dare they interfere with the important work Jesus is doing!

Do they really think the Teacher has time for such trivial things?

BIBLE STUDY

Read Mark 9:33-37; 10:13-16. "The common teachability of children is celebrated throughout Scripture, whereas their occasional rebellion is deplored. Jesus called a child to stand among them to illustrate teachability (Mt 18:2-4). This teachable spirit was among the qualities for which Jesus praised children, welcomed them and likened the kingdom to them (Lk 9:48; 10:21; 18:16). A child's teachable attitude is a model for the Christian's life" (from the *Dictionary of Biblical Imagery*).

[33]They came to Capernaum. When he was in the house, he asked them, "What were you arguing about on the road?" [34]But they kept quiet because on the way they had argued about who was the greatest.

[35]Sitting down, Jesus called the Twelve and said, "Anyone who wants to be first

must be the very last, and the servant of all."

[36]He took a little child whom he placed among them. Taking the child in his arms, he said to them, [37]"Whoever welcomes one of these little children in my name welcomes me; and whoever welcomes me does not welcome me but the one who sent me." (Mk 9:33-37)

[13]People were bringing little children to Jesus for him to place his hands on them, but the disciples rebuked them. [14]When Jesus saw this, he was indignant. He said to them, "Let the little children come to me, and do not hinder them, for the kingdom of God belongs to such as these. [15]Truly I tell you, anyone who will not receive the kingdom of God like a little child will never enter it." [16]And he took the children in his arms, placed his hands on them and blessed them. (Mk 10:13-16)

1. Imagine yourself as one of the disciples. Jesus has just exposed your selfish ambition. Then he summons a child. What do you expect to happen now?

    [Space left intentionally blank in the original book]

2. How do the disciples "want to be first" (9:34-35)?

    [Space left intentionally blank in the original book]

3. In what sense are children "the very last" (9:35)?

[Space left intentionally blank in the original book]

4. When the disciples argue about who is greatest, we might say they are *acting like children*; that is, they are acting in an immature manner. How do the attitudes of children also stand in contrast to the attitudes of the disciples?

[Space left intentionally blank in the original book]

5. How does Jesus associate children with himself and with God the Father (9:37)?

[Space left intentionally blank in the original book]

6. Besides the obvious ways of natural birth and adoption, what are some other ways that people can "welcome" children (9:37)?

[Space left intentionally blank in the original book]

7. *Reread Mark 10:13-16. Rebuked* (10:13) is a strong word. In Mark 9:25 Jesus *rebuked* an evil spirit; in Mark 8:33 he *rebuked* Peter with the words "Get behind me, Satan!" Why do you think the disciples rebuked the parents?

[Space left intentionally blank in the original book]

8. Jesus was *indignant* at the disciples (10:14). Ironically ten of the disciples would soon be *indignant* themselves at the ambition of James and John (Mk 10:41). Besides his own natural compassion, why did Jesus welcome children (10:14-15)?

    [Space left intentionally blank in the original book]

9. Jesus said that "anyone who will not receive the kingdom of God like a little child will never enter it" (10:15). What do you think he meant by *like a little child?*

    [Space left intentionally blank in the original book]

10. Put yourself in the place of one of the disciples as you watch what Jesus does in 10:16. What are your thoughts now?

    [Space left intentionally blank in the original book]

11. Is welcoming children easy or difficult for you? Why?

    [Space left intentionally blank in the original book]

12. What steps can you take to be more open to the children around you?

    [Space left intentionally blank in the original book]

EXPLORING POSSIBILITIES

You may have had a solid Christian upbringing, or you may have known nothing about Christ until you were an adult, or you may come from a background somewhere in between those extremes. In any case, there is no doubt you can recall adults who influenced you in a positive way when you were a child. Your life would be poorer if those people had not been there for you. Now you can be one of those caring and influential adults for a child, perhaps for many children.

- What is your favorite age of children, and why?

    [Space left intentionally blank in the original book]
- Whom do you know, both individuals and organizations, who are doing a good job extending Christ's welcome to children?

    [Space left intentionally blank in the original book]
- What children can you think of who are not being welcomed in your community? in your church?

    [Space left intentionally blank in the original book]
- Think about ways you can extend Christ's welcome to children who are being overlooked. For example:

- host a backyard Bible club
- help with recreation at a neighborhood center
- offer homework help for kids who are struggling in school
- teach thinking skills through chess or other games
- coach or assist with a sport in a summer recreation program
• Visit some of the ongoing children's clubs in your area (not only in churches) and inquire about ways to get involved.

PRAYING INTO THE FUTURE

Thank God for the people who positively influenced you as a child. Pray for the overlooked children in your community. Pray that the Holy Spirit will open your own and other people's eyes and hearts to see these children and to see opportunities to welcome them, remembering that to welcome one of them is to welcome Jesus.

11

Take the Lead

Joshua 1:1-9

PERSONAL NARRATIVE

"We have felt for some time that you were getting too old to continue directing the mission. Therefore, we have decided to retire you."

Eliza Davis George was stunned to hear that she was being discharged from her missionary role in Liberia. At age sixty-six "Mother George" had lived a physically and spiritually demanding life. She suffered from malaria and ulcers on her legs. But she was not ready to abandon Africa.

Eliza Davis, the daughter of former slaves, remembered her mother's longing to see Africa. In her teens Eliza was converted to Christ at a revival meeting. She recalled, "Immediately there seemed to be in my thoughts a longing to do something for Him, but what that 'something' was I did not know."

Eliza earned a teacher's certificate and went on to teach at her college. At a devotional time in 1911, as a professor was praying "all the way around the world," she was filled with a desire to take the gospel to her African brothers and sisters. Her denomination, the National Baptist Convention, was born out of missionary zeal for Africa, but the Texas convention had never sent out a black woman as a pioneering missionary. Eliza convinced the mission board that Africa was her calling from God.

Eliza sailed to Liberia with neither funds nor definite direction. She and another female missionary convinced the Liberian Baptist Convention to allow them to work inland, away from the coast, which already had well-established churches. Together they began a school for native children. Eliza also traveled along rivers by canoe, accompanied by an interpreter, telling people about Jesus.

After two years Eliza learned that a split in her denomination would lead to her being replaced by other missionaries. Not only did she lack the funds to return to the United States, she desperately wanted to stay in Africa. At this point C. Thompson George reappeared in Eliza's life. He was a well-traveled and well-educated man of African ancestry. He had once proposed marriage to Eliza and she had turned him down. Now he promised Eliza that if she would marry him, he would help her start a new mission in a dangerous tribal area in the Liberian interior. Nearly forty years old, Eliza consented to marry C. Thompson. It was a difficult marriage, as he turned out to be personally unstable.

C. Thompson and "Mother George" received only meager financial support from American churches. They founded Kelton Mission, a school and farm, with no charge for tuition or food. They rescued girls from child marriages, saw young Liberians converted to Christ and a church established, and sent several to the United States for higher education. When C. Thompson died in 1939, Mother George continued the work with the aid of young Liberian Christian leaders.

When Mother George was sixty-six, officials from the National Baptist Convention came to Liberia and insisted that she return with them to Texas to rest. On the boat crossing the Atlantic, they told Mother George that she would not be allowed to return and that Kelton would be moved from its remote location closer to a road for future automobile traffic.

Mother George was not ready to quit. She told herself, "The Convention didn't call me; God Almighty called me." She would take the initiative and go back to Liberia on her own. In the United States she began a letter-writing campaign and booked a heavy schedule of meetings to raise support for her new mission. When she tried to return to Liberia at age sixty-nine, the shipping company told her she was too old for the voyage, so she flew in an airplane for the first time in her life, "determined that my bones will bleach on African soil."

Mother George ventured further into the Liberian interior where there were no schools. She supervised the building of a mission in the "devil bush," a "cursed place" where no native villager would farm. She visited villages where the people had never heard about Christ. The president of Liberia decorated her for "distinguished and sacrificial services" in 1972. She died at age one hundred still holding up her light for Christ.

- What is your reaction to Mother George's determination to continue her ministry in Africa after her mission board let her go?

    [Space left intentionally blank in the original book]

- When have you had to take the lead in a project because others didn't see its importance? What happened as a result?

    [Space left intentionally blank in the original book]

CONNECTING WITH A BIBLE CHARACTER

Joshua blinks, shakes his head, blinks again. What did Moses just say? Moses isn't going to lead the people of Israel into the Promised Land?

Everyone knows Moses can't live forever, but surely he will take them across the Jordan River into Canaan and be their rock of stability while they get established. But Moses says the Lord will not allow it. What are they going to do without Moses? How can this huge mass of people enter the Promised Land with no visible human leader at their head?

What's this? Moses says that as he surveyed the land God would give them, he asked the Lord to appoint a man to take his place, "to go out and come in before them, one who will lead them out and bring them in, so the Lord's people will not be like sheep without a shepherd." And the Lord told him to appoint Joshua! "Take Joshua son of Nun, a man in whom is the spirit, and lay your hand on him."

Joshua can't believe it. He has certainly been close to Moses all these years. He was one of the twelve trusted spies sent into Canaan to look things over in advance. When ten of the others came back and said "We can't do it. The Canaanites are too strong for us," only Joshua and Caleb urged the people to go ahead, believing that God would give them success.

Joshua was a vigorous young man then, but that was forty years ago. *Am I up to this new job?* he wonders. *Of course Moses didn't think he was up to the job either, when God called him from the burning bush. But can I ever hope to be a leader like Moses?*

Joshua doesn't have much time to think things over. Moses is summoning Eleazar the priest and calling all the people together. The three of them—Joshua, Moses and Eleazar—stand before the great assembly of Israelites.

Trembling inside, Joshua closes his eyes and feels the strong hands of Moses touching his head. These same wiry hands once held the staff of God over the dividing waters of the Red Sea.

Aaron and Hur once held up those hands while Joshua battled the Amalekites on the plain below. Now Moses' hands are imparting authority, commissioning Joshua to lead the Israelites into Canaan.

Moses' voice reveals his age, but it's still strong as he tells the people, "The Lord your God himself will cross over ahead of you. He will destroy these nations before you, and you will take possession of their land. Joshua also will cross over ahead of you, as the Lord said."

Joshua stands up straight and opens his eyes. The Lord will cross the Jordan and go into Canaan *ahead* of them. Then Joshua will lead the people across. The Lord is going first! How can he be afraid now? Joshua still trembles a little, but he is ready to step into leadership.

BIBLE STUDY

Read Joshua 1:1-9. For background on Joshua's leadership and his relationship with Moses, read Exodus 17:8-16; 24:12-18; 33:7-11; Numbers 13:1–14:38; 27:12-23; and Deuteronomy 31:1-8.

[1]After the death of Moses the servant of the LORD, the Lord said to Joshua son of Nun, Moses' aide: [2]"Moses my servant is dead. Now then, you and all these people, get ready to cross the Jordan River into the land I am about to give to them—to the Israelites. [3]I will give you every place where you set your foot, as I

promised Moses. [4]Your territory will extend from the desert to Lebanon, and from the great river, the Euphrates—all the Hittite country—to the Mediterranean Sea in the west. [5]No one will be able to stand against you all the days of your life. As I was with Moses, so I will be with you; I will never leave you nor forsake you. [6]Be strong and courageous, because you will lead these people to inherit the land I swore to their ancestors to give them.

[7]Be strong and very courageous. Be careful to obey all the law my servant Moses gave you; do not turn from it to the right or to the left, that you may be successful wherever you go. [8]Keep this Book of the Law always on your lips; meditate on it day and night, so that you may be careful to do everything written in it. Then you will be prosperous and successful. [9]Have I not commanded you? Be strong and courageous. Do not be afraid; do not be discouraged, for the LORD your God will be with you wherever you go."

1. What is the dominant mood of this passage?
   [Space left intentionally blank in the original book]
2. Put yourself in Joshua's place. Moses, leader of Israel for forty years, hero of the exodus from Egypt, is dead. You are his successor. Your job is to lead a huge populace into

a new country and conquer its powerful inhabitants. What are your hopes?

[Space left intentionally blank in the original book]

3. Still thinking of yourself as Joshua, what are your anxieties?

[Space left intentionally blank in the original book]

4. Speaking as yourself now, do you share any of Joshua's possible anxieties about leadership?

[Space left intentionally blank in the original book]

5. How do you feel about leadership opportunities? Do you welcome them? Deliberately seek them out? Avoid them? Take them on, but reluctantly? Flee from them? And why?

[Space left intentionally blank in the original book]

6. What are some good and bad motivations for desiring leadership?

[Space left intentionally blank in the original book]

7. What areas of expertise do you have that could be useful in guiding or motivating others?

[Space left intentionally blank in the original book]

8. What promises does the Lord make to the Israelites, whom Joshua would lead (vv. 2-4)?

[Space left intentionally blank in the original book]

9. What promises does the Lord make to Joshua himself (vv. 5-9)?

[Space left intentionally blank in the original book]

10. Joshua is instructed to stay faithful to the book of God's law (vv. 7-8). What is the connection between obeying God and successful leadership?

[Space left intentionally blank in the original book]

11. What ultimately gave Joshua confidence to lead the people (v. 9)?

[Space left intentionally blank in the original book]

12. What gives you confidence to lead?

[Space left intentionally blank in the original book]

EXPLORING POSSIBILITIES

Look again at your response to question 12 above. Maybe you named several factors that give you confidence to lead others. Or maybe you answered "Nothing!" Whether or not you feel qualified, you can be sure that when God puts you in a leadership position, he will equip and enable you for the job.

- "Have I not commanded you? Be strong and courageous. Do not be terrified; do not be discouraged, for the LORD your God will be with you wherever you go" (Josh 1:9). God spoke those words to Joshua on the bank of the Jordan River. If God spoke those words directly to you today, what task or responsibility would he be talking about?

    [Space left intentionally blank in the original book]

- Write down some endeavors that you think are important but others do not consider important. In the face of others' indifference, why are you still convinced that these things are worth doing?

    [Space left intentionally blank in the original book]

- Choose one of the endeavors you wrote down and focus on it. Imagine yourself starting a new effort to take on this issue. Picture your goal being achieved. What does it look like? What is the best thing about the results?

    [Space left intentionally blank in the original book]

- Go back to the start of the endeavor you chose. What would be your first step to get things moving?

    [Space left intentionally blank in the original book]

- How might you enlist other people or at least one other person?

    [Space left intentionally blank in the original book]

PRAYING INTO THE FUTURE

Offer yourself to the Lord for the task and responsibility of leadership. Ask him to purify your motives from self-centeredness. If you tend to leap blindly into leadership, pray for humility and discretion. If you tend to duck leadership, pray for confidence in God's leading and enabling. Claim the promise of Joshua 1:9 as your own.

12

Welcome the Stranger

Acts 8:26-40

PERSONAL NARRATIVE

"Good morning. Are you open today?"

The Taiwanese woman was not phoning a store or an office. She was calling our house. A heavy snowstorm had closed the schools and made driving difficult. We did not expect the members of our multinational English conversation group to show up that morning.

But yes, we were "open." And all of them showed up: women from Japan, Taiwan and Korea, *and* their preschool children, *and* their older children who had the day off from school. We all met in our rather small basement. The adults had our usual conversation time while the children played in an adjoining space.

The conversation group met at our house during a break in English classes for internationals at a local church. We had investigated teaching at the church and there were no openings, but during the January-February break the teachers were happy to have us host a group to help the students get more practice in speaking.

One woman from Korea, a Christian believer, lived in a townhouse complex near our house. For two years we had ridden our bikes past those townhouses, which were obviously filled with internationals. We had prayed for an opening there to help people with English. Surely this Korean woman was our God-given contact!

Just before classes resumed at the church, one of the teachers held a one-day cooking class. There we asked our Korean friend if she would be willing to host a conversation group at her house. We were disappointed when she did not seem interested. But another woman standing nearby overheard us and spoke up. "I live in one of those houses and I'd like to do that!"

Within a week she had organized a group of three Korean women who wanted to practice English one morning a week. They soon recruited a fourth person. When one of them went back to Korea, they recruited two more. Each week we meet in a different home, but the format is the same. For an hour and a half we gather around a kitchen table, enjoy snacks (both Korean and American), and converse in English about anything and everything.

We are much older than any of these women. We could be their grandparents and the great-grandparents of their children, but the age difference doesn't matter. We are native English speakers and that's what is important to them.

Recently one of the women said she has started religious instruction. She explained, "My life is good, I have everything I want, but still sometimes I feel empty in my heart." Our discussion led to spending part of our time for five weeks studying what the Bible says about creation, the Fall and forgiveness through Christ.

The women would often say, "Our friends envy us. They wish they had a group where they could practice speaking English." With five Koreans plus us two Americans, we had reached the capacity of their kitchen tables. We had to think about starting a second group.

Then one day something unexpected happened: a ready-made group appeared. One of the women who hosts our group said a friend was coming by to meet us. The "friend" turned out to be *three* people who burst in the door shaking ice from their coats—it had started to sleet—and exclaiming, "We are so happy to have someone to practice English!" In only a few minutes we lined up a second weekly conversation group.

So far, our prayers for a contact in the townhouse complex have been answered nine times over. We expect many more such answers to prayer in the future.

We are interested in foreigners not because they are needier or more interesting than other people. It's because we know what it's like to land in a foreign country, not knowing the language and with very little money. We know what it's like to be unable to make ourselves understood in the market or over the phone.

We know what it's like to be evicted from our apartment for reasons we didn't understand and have to move all our belongings across the city in winter with no car. We have been those foreigners.

- What different nationalities of people are you aware of in your community? Why are they there?

    [Space left intentionally blank in the original book]

- What experiences in your life help you understand what foreigners experience coming to your community?

    [Space left intentionally blank in the original book]

CONNECTING WITH A BIBLE CHARACTER

The African man squints at the Greek letters on the scroll. The bouncing chariot wheels make reading difficult. He grumbles to the driver, who only shrugs.

> *At this time in history the name* Ethiopia *did not refer to modern Ethiopia. It was "the ancient name of the territory S[outh] of Egypt, corresponding roughly to the present Sudan." In the Bible it is also called* Cush.

The horses are walking at a sedate pace. *It's this rough desert road,* the man thinks, *this desolate track from Jerusalem to Gaza. Can't be helped; this is my most direct route home to Ethiopia.* For some time they have seen only one other traveler, a Jewish man following on foot some distance behind them. The Ethiopian is grateful that his position as treasurer to the queen merits him a chariot for travel.

> *"From the time of Ptolemy II (308-246 B.C.) the kingdom [Ethiopia] became partly Hellenized. Greeks had visited there since 665 B.C.... That a high official in the queen's court—indeed, the treasurer of her kingdom—should be able to read the Greek roll of Isaiah is not a problem. How he had the roll, if he was neither a Jew nor a proselyte, may be a problem; yet a court official could find a way."*

The Ethiopian is glad he was able to obtain this scroll of the prophet Isaiah during his stay in Jerusalem, where he went to worship God at the Jewish temple. Thank God for those translators who rendered the Scriptures of the Jews into the Greek language. Right now, however, he wishes for more than a translation. He wants an interpreter. The words of Isaiah fascinate him and mystify him. He continues to read aloud:

He was led like a sheep to the slaughter,
and as a lamb before the shearer is silent,
so he did not open his mouth.

> *"Though taught along with reading aloud in modern times, the skill of reading silently was not developed in antiquity; those who could read nearly always read aloud."*

Of course I understand the humility of sheep, but who is this mysterious " he" whom Isaiah compares to a sheep? What does it all mean?

"Do you understand what you are reading?"

The Ethiopian almost drops the scroll. That voice came out of nowhere. A man is walking alongside the chariot! It's the Jew who was following behind them. He's puffing a little. He must have run hard to catch up.

The driver, afraid of robbers, raises his whip to urge the horses into a run. His master stops him. Somehow this stranger doesn't look dangerous. Why would a Jew ask an African if he understands what he is reading? Why would it matter? Intrigued, the African invites the Israelite to ride with him in the chariot. The stranger introduces himself as Philip. A Jew with a Greek name. Interesting.

Immediately the Jew with the Greek name and the African are engaged in a deep discussion of a passage from the prophet Isaiah.

BIBLE STUDY

Read Acts 8:26-40. For background read Acts 8:1-25. Philip, one of the original seven deacons of the church, had left Jerusalem because of the persecution which arose after the martyrdom of Stephen. He had already bridged a cultural gap by preaching in Samaria before the Lord sent him onto the road to Gaza.

[26]Now an angel of the Lord said to Philip, "Go south to the road—the desert road—that goes down from Jerusalem to Gaza." [27]So he started out, and on his way he met an Ethiopian eunuch, an important official in charge of all the treasury of the Kandake (which means "queen of the Ethiopians"). This man had gone to Jerusalem to worship, [28]and on his way home was sitting in his chariot reading the Book of Isaiah the prophet. [29]The Spirit told Philip, "Go to that chariot and stay near it."

[30]Then Philip ran up to the chariot and heard the man reading Isaiah the prophet. "Do you understand what you are reading?" Philip asked.

[31]"How can I," he said, "unless someone explains it to me?" So he invited Philip to come up and sit with him.

[32]This is the passage of Scripture the eunuch was reading:

"He was led like a sheep to the slaughter,
and as a lamb before its shearer is silent,
so he did not open his mouth.
[33]In his humiliation he was deprived of justice.
Who can speak of his descendants?
For his life was taken from the earth."

[34]The eunuch asked Philip, "Tell me, please, who is the prophet talking about, himself or someone else?" [35]Then Philip began with that very passage of Scripture and told him the good news about Jesus. [36]As they traveled along the road, they came to some water and the eunuch said, "Look, here is water. What can stand in the way of my being baptized?" ... [38]And he gave orders to stop the chariot. Then both Philip and the eunuch went down into the water and Philip baptized him. [39]When they came up out of the water, the Spirit of the Lord suddenly took Philip away, and the eunuch did not see him again, but went on his way rejoicing. [40]Philip, however, appeared at Azotus and traveled about, preaching the gospel in all the towns until he reached Caesarea.

1. Persecution had scattered most of the Christians from Jerusalem, including Philip, one of the original seven deacons. How

does Philip wind up on the road to Gaza in the vicinity of the Ethiopian's chariot (vv. 26-29)?

[Space left intentionally blank in the original book]

2. What cultural barriers would stand between Philip and the Ethiopian?

[Space left intentionally blank in the original book]

3. How does the Ethiopian show a willingness to be helped by Philip (vv. 30-34)?

[Space left intentionally blank in the original book]

4. Whom do you know, or whom have you known, who has shown what seems to be an unlikely interest in the Bible?

[Space left intentionally blank in the original book]

5. How does Philip show wisdom and sensitivity in his dealings with the Ethiopian (vv. 30-31, 35)?

[Space left intentionally blank in the original book]

> *In the Law, God instructed Israel to care for aliens (foreigners) and treat them fairly because the Israelites had themselves been foreigners in Egypt. For example:*
> *"He defends the cause of the fatherless and the widow, and loves the foreigner*

> *residing among you, giving them food and clothing. And you are to love those who are foreigners, for you yourselves were foreigners in Egypt" (Deut 10:18-19).*
>
> *"When a foreigner resides among you in your land, do not mistreat him. The foreigner residing among you must be treated as your native-born. Love them as yourself, for you were foreigners in Egypt. I am the LORD your God" (Lev 19:33-34).*
>
> *"Do not oppress a foreigner; you yourselves know how it feels to be foreigners, because you were foreigners in Egypt" (Ex 23:9).*

6. What contacts have you had with the foreigners in your own area? (We use the word *foreigners* because not all internationals are *immigrants*. For example, the Korean women in the Personal Narrative above are here temporarily while their physician husbands do research at Mayo Clinic.)

    [Space left intentionally blank in the original book]

7. What are the prevailing attitudes toward foreigners in your community?

    [Space left intentionally blank in the original book]

8. What are your own attitudes toward foreigners in your community?

[Space left intentionally blank in the original book]

9. Recall a time when you had "the heart of a stranger," not on a brief trip to a foreign country but as a persistent emotional state. Who acted as a "Philip" for you, and how?

[Space left intentionally blank in the original book]

10. Do you know of any Christians who are acting as "Philips" for foreigners in your area? What are they doing?

[Space left intentionally blank in the original book]

11. How were both the Ethiopian and Philip blessed as a result of their conversation and travel together (vv. 36-40)?

[Space left intentionally blank in the original book]

> *"The pentateuchal laws regarding aliens demonstrate a clear humanitarian concern, including guarantees of evenhanded justice without prejudice to their status, fair payment of wages, gleaning rights to the leftover harvest, other provision of food from the triennial tithe, inclusion in feasts alongside the orphan and widow, and inclusion in the sabbath rest. The call to treat the alien with justice and special consideration was motivated by Israelite*

> *identification with the vulnerable position of the alien, which had been such a formative part of their own experience."*

12. When you think of being involved with people of a very different culture from your own, what are your anxieties? What good possibilities do you see?
    [Space left intentionally blank in the original book]

EXPLORING POSSIBILITIES

The Ethiopian in Acts 8 was already puzzling over the Scriptures. He welcomed Philip's guidance. Not all foreigners will present you with such an immediate opportunity to study the Bible. But they are puzzling over other things—how life in your country works and especially how they can survive and thrive here.

Explore opportunities to get more involved with the foreigners in your area, whether immigrants or temporary visitors. Here are some ideas for breaking the ice:
- Most foreigners welcome any opportunity to practice speaking English. Make conversation in the grocery checkout line or at the bus stop. On a more structured basis, a conversation group takes no more expertise

than the ability to speak English and a friendly attitude.
- Ask a foreign neighbor or coworker to teach you to cook a native dish. Share the meal in either your home or the foreigner's home.
- If you have children in school, it is likely they have foreign classmates. Encourage them to befriend these children.
- If you homeschool your children and know a foreigner who dresses differently from you, create a cross-cultural lesson by inviting the foreigner to come to your home and explain the differences in apparel.
- If your community has an adult literacy program, it's likely some of the learners are foreigners who are literate in their own language but not in English. You can help one person with far-reaching results.
- Many North American schools are struggling to cope with the influx of students from non-English-speaking homes. They welcome volunteers to help with schoolwork. Your public library may offer similar opportunities after school.
- Consider who else in your community might be thought of as foreigners, not because of nationality but because they do not fit into the mainstream of society. Explore ways to welcome them also.

PRAYING INTO THE FUTURE

Pray that the Holy Spirit will break down barriers and build bridges between cultures in your community. Pray that God will open eyes to really see the people doing service jobs or in other settings where they are easily overlooked. Pray that your church will be a welcoming place for all people and a "house of prayer for all nations" (Is 56:7).

13

Look to the Future

Luke 1:5-25, 57-66

PERSONAL NARRATIVE

We often see them together, an unlikely pair, yet in another way a perfect match. He is Jhon Diego Riascos, a twenty-nineyear-old former Colombian soldier. She is Sister Joseen Vogt, age eighty-eight, four feet nine inches tall. Four days a week you can see them intensely studying together at an adult education center.

Jhon Riascos was engaged in the war on drug trafficking in Colombia when a grenade went off in his face, rendering him blind and severely disfigured. He is undergoing a long, difficult series of facial reconstruction surgeries at Mayo Clinic. His stay in the U.S. is sponsored by the foundation United for Colombia.

Sister Joseen's route to this place is longer and more convoluted. She was fifty-two years old, teaching biology in Australia, when a photograph revolutionized her life. On vacation in Hong Kong she took a picture of one of the city's floating restaurants. When she looked at the picture later, in the corner she saw something—or rather someone—she had missed. A little girl, a beggar, stared into the camera. Sister Joseen recalls, "She was saying to me, 'What are you going to do for me?' That's where I learned that I must go to developing countries and help the poor. God wanted me somewhere else."

"Somewhere else" has included Sierra Leone in West Africa, Cambodia and the Philippines. Sister Joseen is an educational innovator. In Sierra Leone she taught English to two people who were blind. She had used hands-on learning in science classes, and she carried over the theory to English. If blind people could learn Braille, she reasoned, why couldn't they learn a different language through their hands as well? Using tactile techniques she was amazed at the progress her blind students made.

Back in the United States, Sister Joseen learned that a tutor was being sought for Jhon Riascos. She was hired and began to teach Riascos through tactile methods, including her own alphabet crafted from heavy cord and cardboard. She recalls the day she put a pen in Jhon's hand and with his other hand had him feel the letters P-E-N. When he pronounced the English word *pen,* the expression on his war-damaged face turned to joy.

Sister Joseen sees her life as *before* and *after* that Hong Kong photograph. She burned her journals from the *before* part of her life and has written three volumes about the *after.* She

explains, "I'm led wherever. That's my whole belief. There's no need for me to plan, because I'll be led."
- Do you know an older person who has not succumbed to living in the past but is focused on the future?

    [Space left intentionally blank in the original book]
- How does the person's forward-looking attitude affect his or her everyday life?

    [Space left intentionally blank in the original book]

CONNECTING WITH A BIBLE CHARACTER

Zechariah trembles as he enters the curtained Holy Place in the temple in Jerusalem. As a descendant of Aaron and a priest of the Lord, he has the duty today to burn the incense in this sacred spot. The only place more sacred is the Holy of Holies where only the high priest can go once a year.

In the flickering light from the seven-branched lampstand, gold glimmers all around Zechariah. The walls of the Holy Place are overlaid with gold. A gold table holds twelve loaves of bread. The altar of incense is gold, and it glows with its own charcoal fire. The smoky atmosphere makes Zechariah's eyes water. He blinks and coughs. His mind wanders outside the temple where the air is clear. Outside in the courtyards, crowds of people are praying.

He thinks of his wife Elizabeth. They have had a good life together. With so many priests living around Jerusalem, he seldom serves in the temple. Together they tend a small farm in the hill country. But they often wonder who will take care of them when they can't work anymore. They have no children, and both of them are—as he likes to put it tactfully—*well along in years.*

Zechariah chuckles a little and catches himself. He should be serious here. *Perhaps I should pray for a child,* he thinks. *No, that's ridiculous. It's too late, years too late.*

> "To be childless was economically and socially disastrous: economically, because parents had no one to support them in old age, ... socially, because in the law barrenness was sometimes a judgment for sin, and many people assumed the worst possible cause of a problem."

Certainly Zechariah can utter a prayer of gratitude that he is here. There are so many priests serving in rotation that, even at his age, this is the first time he has ever had the opportunity to enter the Holy Place to burn the incense.

> "According to Luke, Zechariah is a priest in the order of Abijah—a designation reflecting the division of the priests into groups due to their excessive numbers.... Each group served in the Temple twice each year for one week. During their Temple service, duties were divided among the priests by lot, with the greatest honor falling to the one chosen to enter the Temple and burn incense. Luke narrates that Zechariah was chosen for this exceptional duty, which could be performed by a priest only once in his lifetime."

Zechariah approaches the incense altar and sprinkles the fragrant powder onto the glowing coals. Bright sparks flare up. The heavy, spicy aroma makes him lightheaded. Very lightheaded. He's seeing things! It looks like the form of a man, but it can't be; he is alone here. Isn't he? No, Zechariah isn't alone, and now he is terrified. He has never seen an angel, but somehow he knows that is what he sees standing beside the altar of incense. He can hardly breathe, and not because of the smoke.

"Do not be afraid, Zechariah. Your prayer has been heard."

What prayer? My prayer of thanks? Why would God send an angel to tell me that?

"Your wife Elizabeth will bear you a son, and you are to give him the name John."

That's strange, no one in our family has that name ... What! Elizabeth have a son? This must be a dream! The angel says more about this supposed son, but Zechariah can't buy it. He asks, "How can I be sure?"

A few seconds later, he wishes he hadn't asked. He can't talk! He turns to leave, to escape this alarming place. But how is he going to explain? How will he tell anybody what happened here?

BIBLE STUDY

Read Luke 1:5-25, 57-66. In the events surrounding the birth of Christ, angels helped people look toward the future with faith and anticipation. Here Gabriel appeared to Zechariah, father of John the Baptist. Gabriel also appeared to Mary to tell her that she would give birth to Jesus (Lk 1:26-38). An unnamed angel reassured Joseph that he should go ahead and marry Mary (Mt 1:18-25). An angel—accompanied by many more—announced to the shepherds that the Savior was born (Lk 2:8-12).

> [5]In the time of Herod king of Judea there was a priest named Zechariah, who belonged to the priestly division of Abijah; his wife Elizabeth was also a descendant of Aaron. [6]Both of them were righteous in the sight of God, observing all the Lord's commands and decrees blamelessly. [7]But they were childless because Elizabeth was

not able to conceive, and they were both very old.

[8]Once when Zechariah's division was on duty and he was serving as priest before God, [9]he was chosen by lot, according to the custom of the priesthood, to go into the temple of the Lord and burn incense. [10]And when the time for the burning of incense came, all the assembled worshipers were praying outside.

[11]Then an angel of the Lord appeared to him, standing at the right side of the altar of incense. [12]When Zechariah saw him, he was startled and was gripped with fear. [13]But the angel said to him: "Do not be afraid, Zechariah; your prayer has been heard. Your wife Elizabeth will bear you a son, and you are to call him John. [14]He will be a joy and delight to you, and many will rejoice because of his birth, [15]for he will be great in the sight of the Lord. He is never to take wine or other fermented drink, and he will be filled with the Holy Spirit even before he is born. [16]He will bring back many of the people of Israel to the Lord their God. [17]And he will go on before the Lord, in the spirit and power of Elijah, to turn the hearts of the parents to their children and the disobedient to the wisdom of the righteous—to make ready a people prepared for the Lord."

[18]Zechariah asked the angel, "How can I be sure of this? I am an old man and my wife is well along in years."

[19]The angel said to him, "I am Gabriel. I stand in the presence of God, and I have been sent to speak to you and to tell you this good news. [20]And now you will be silent and not able to speak until the day this happens, because you did not believe my words, which will come true at their appointed time."

[21]Meanwhile, the people were waiting for Zechariah and wondering why he stayed so long in the temple. [22]When he came out, he could not speak to them. They realized he had seen a vision in the temple, for he kept making signs to them but remained unable to speak.

[23]When his time of service was completed, he returned home. After this his wife Elizabeth became pregnant and for five months remained in seclusion. [25]"The Lord has done this for me," she said. "In these days he has shown his favor and taken away my disgrace among the people." (Lk 1:5-25)

[57]When it was time for Elizabeth to have her baby, she gave birth to a son. [58]Her neighbors and relatives heard that the Lord had shown her great mercy, and they shared her joy.

[59]On the eighth day they came to circumcise the child, and they were going

to name him after his father Zechariah, [60]but his mother spoke up and said, "No! He is to be called John."

[61]They said to her, "There is no one among your relatives who has that name." [62]Then they made signs to his father, to find out what he would like to name the child. [63]He asked for a writing tablet, and to everyone's astonishment he wrote, "His name is John." [64]Immediately his mouth was opened and his tongue set free, and he began to speak, praising God. [65]All the neighbors were filled with awe, and throughout the hill country of Judea people were talking about all these things. [66]Everyone who heard this wondered about it, asking, "What then is this child going to be?" For the Lord's hand was with him. (Lk 1:57-66)

1. At the beginning of this account, what reasons do Zechariah and Elizabeth have to focus on the past rather than on the future?

    [Space left intentionally blank in the original book]

2. What reasons do you have to focus on the past rather than on the future?

    [Space left intentionally blank in the original book]

3. How do you see God's sovereignty in placing Zechariah in the temple at this moment (vv. 5-10)?

[Space left intentionally blank in the original book]

4. Imagine that you are Zechariah at the moment of verses 11-12. What do you feel and think?

[Space left intentionally blank in the original book]

5. What does the angel predict about the son to be born to Zechariah and Elizabeth (vv. 13-17)?

[Space left intentionally blank in the original book]

6. Despite the appearance and message of the angel, Zechariah is still dubious (v. 18). What do you think of his doubts? What doubts of yours are similar to Zechariah's?

[Space left intentionally blank in the original book]

7. How does the angel respond with both a rebuke and a promise (vv. 19-20)?

[Space left intentionally blank in the original book]

8. In their old age how is Zechariah and Elizabeth's attention abruptly turned to the future (vv. 21-25)?

[Space left intentionally blank in the original book]

9. *Reread Luke 1:57-66.* How does Zechariah show his faithfulness to the angel's promise (vv. 57-64)?

[Space left intentionally blank in the original book]

> *"Casting incense on the heated altar of incense normally took little time, after which the priest emerged immediately. The delay here may have troubled the crowds; perhaps they thought Zechariah had been disrespectful and struck dead, or that something else had gone wrong."*

10. What do Elizabeth and Zechariah have to look forward to now (vv. 65-66)?

[Space left intentionally blank in the original book]

11. In what ways has the Lord proved his faithfulness to you in times of prolonged doubt and uncertainty? Respond in praise to him for his great faithfulness.

[Space left intentionally blank in the original book]

> *Zechariah and Elizabeth's son John was the fulfillment of the prophecy of Isaiah 40:3-5. He became known as John the Baptist. He called people to repentance*

> *and announced the coming of Jesus Christ (Lk 3:1-20).*

EXPLORING POSSIBILITIES

It would appear that Zechariah and Elizabeth had a well-defined idea of what their future would look like. Then God intervened and made their future radically different from anything they could imagine. Not only would they become parents at last, they would be the parents of the forerunner of the Messiah, and their names would live forever in Scripture.

- What is your reaction to the idea that God might rearrange your future as radically as he did that of Elizabeth and Zechariah?

  [Space left intentionally blank in the original book]

- Would you say you are a future-oriented or a past-oriented person? Why do you answer as you do?

  [Space left intentionally blank in the original book]

- If you would like to see one thing happen in your future here on earth, what would it be?

  [Space left intentionally blank in the original book]

- Look ahead to the next section of this book, appropriately titled "What's Next?" There you will find resources to help you take stock of your interests, experiences and abilities and match them up with possible opportunities to stay actively involved in serving people. The format of "What's Next?" is somewhat different from the other thirteen sessions in this book. It is designed for individuals to work through on their own.

PRAYING INTO THE FUTURE

No matter whether you look toward the future with apprehension or with anticipation, commit your future to the Lord. Pray for God's guidance for the course(s) of action you will pursue. Pray for at least one colleague to work with you. Thank God that you can have confidence in him that no matter what your age or life situation, there is still much you can do to serve him.

Conclusion

What's Next?

This final section has a different format from the previous thirteen chapters. It is designed for individuals to work through on their own.

Take your time going through this section. Feel free to go through different parts of it several times. Some material in this chapter is adapted from chapter two of Gordon T. Smith's book *Courage and Calling: Embracing Your God-Given Potential.*

In Romans 12:3, Paul urges us to evaluate ourselves in a godly way: "For by the grace given me I say to every one of you: Do not think of yourself more highly than you ought, but rather think of yourself with sober judgment, in accordance with the faith God has distributed to each of you."

We gain a sober judgment of ourselves, Smith suggests, when we respond to four questions:

- What are my gifts and abilities?

    [Space left intentionally blank in the original book]

- What is the deepest desire of my heart?

    [Space left intentionally blank in the original book]

- Where do I personally sense the needs of the world and feel the brokenness in God's creation?

    [Space left intentionally blank in the original book]

- What is my unique personality or temperament?

    [Space left intentionally blank in the original book]

We will work our way through those four questions, maintaining focus on the future, with the aim of uncovering God's direction for what's next.

MY GIFTS AND ABILITIES

You may have heard it said that "God is looking not for ability but for availability." It is more accurate to say that "God is looking for people of ability who will make their ability available to God."

Take stock of your abilities which you can make available to God. Be honest. Don't hide your skills behind false modesty. Ask your friends and family about the gifts they have observed in you. They may have seen qualities you never realized you possessed.

As a guide for evaluating your gifts and abilities, write down your responses to the following questions. Expect some overlap in your answers. You can also use the suggestions under

Exploring Possibilities in chapter eight. While the list in that chapter is meant to help you find alternative ways to earn money, it can also jump-start your ideas for volunteer efforts.

- What do I know how to do?

    Examples: use desktop publishing, play the clarinet, speak Arabic, plant a garden, organize a group of people to accomplish a task, run a power boat, make great cinnamon rolls, play chess, make a house spotlessly clean, conduct myself in a job interview, listen without interrupting.

    [Space left intentionally blank in the original book]

- What skills have I developed in my work life, including homemaking skills?

    Examples: managing people, small engine repair, budgeting, data entry, medical knowledge, public speaking, dealing with unhappy customers, bookkeeping, caring for small children, stocking shelves, driving a bus, roofing, plumbing.

    [Space left intentionally blank in the original book]

- What skills have I already used in volunteering?

    Examples: construction, coaching sports, fundraising, doing publicity, leading a youth group, keeping minutes of organizations, giving rides to people who don't drive, greeting newcomers at church, painting, financial counseling.

[Space left intentionally blank in the original book]

- What are my hobbies, pastimes and interests?

    Examples: running, rock collecting, racquetball, wood carving, singing or playing in music groups, photography, caving, antique cars, astronomy, gardening, motorcycles, square dancing, cooking, genealogical research, archery.

    [Space left intentionally blank in the original book]

MY DEEPEST DESIRES

Look back through the Exploring Possibilities sections in the previous thirteen chapters. Which efforts that you read about really grabbed you and stirred your emotions and your imagination? The ones that touched you most deeply can reveal the changes that your heart longs to see happen in the world. They may also lead you to think of a need that has not been mentioned.

Gordon Smith urges us to ask, "If I could only be one thing and do one thing with my life, what would I want it to be?" As you consider that query, be careful not to narrow your focus so drastically that you lock yourself into a single course of action. The point is not to do one *activity*, but to have one *goal*.

Reflect on what specific hurt in the world you would most like to see eased, what specific lack you would most like to see supplied, what specific trouble you would most like to see resolved. Be open to new ideas. You may find yourself developing a passion for a cause that you have previously ignored or overlooked.

THE NEEDS I SEE

When Sandy was a student at Greenville College, a chapel speaker (name long forgotten) said, "It is more Christian to do a few things well than a great many things in a mediocre way."

So much cries out to be done. Your mailbox overflows with calls to action, from refugee settlement to evangelizing university students, from medical missions to well drilling. Every cause presents itself as the most urgent, but you can't—and shouldn't—try to respond to them all.

As we have investigated creative things older people are doing, we have been most impressed by the simplest efforts of one person or one small group of people, serving in an area overlooked by others.

Carole Perkins is one woman who saw a deficiency and said, "I can do something about that." At age sixty-one Carole had served on overseas mission trips, lost two husbands and coped with cancer. When the only café closed in her tiny town of LeRoy, Minnesota, Carole thought the town's residents still needed a place to gather and talk. She persuaded Bethany Bible Church to open their doors at 6:00 a.m. weekdays for anyone to come and have morning coffee for free. Now Carole arrives before 6:00 each morning to get the coffee started. All kinds of people show up to sit around tables and chat. Low-key Christian music plays in the background. People talk about the news of the world, what's going on in their own lives, the books they're reading. And they do not fail to notice when one of the regulars is missing.

> *"We all see the brokenness of the world through the very particular lenses of our own eyes and heart. Often we miss our vocation because our sense of the needs of the world is informed and shaped by the expectations of others. Sometimes preachers or speakers outline the needs of the world in a way that is very compelling. They describe the needs in a way that communicates that if we really cared we would respond according to their expectations.... But we must act on our own vision for a needy world—a vision informed by our personal reading of the Scriptures, a reading that is sustained by the witness of the Spirit to our own heart.... The need does not determine the call."*

Look for something that needs to be done, which nobody else is doing, where you are moved to say "I can do something about that."

MY PERSONALITY

"Works well without supervision." "Takes initiative." "Self-starter." Did you always get those boxes checked on job evaluations? You will do fine in a volunteer position where you can plan your own work and set your own schedule. You will be frustrated if you serve on a large committee which has to reach a consensus before any aspect of a project can move forward.

If you are a detail person, you will be outstanding in a role that calls for close attention and precision. You will flounder, and may even be unpopular, in a "vision casting" group of big-picture people who are thinking ten years ahead.

A candid assessment of your own personality will steer you toward the right endeavors and keep you clear of the wrong ones.

Shortly after the breakup of the Soviet Union, we taught English in Ukraine for a year through Educational Services International (now www.teachoverseas.org). We were told that the job required "a high tolerance for ambiguity." In other words, if life must be orderly and predictable and you have to be in control, don't sign up to teach in the former USSR. We did all right in Ukraine because decades of self-employment had accustomed us to unpredictability, but we were still grateful for the warning.

You may wish to take the Myers Briggs assessment (www.myersbriggs.org) or another personality assessment. You can also ask your friends and family for their opinions, as long as you're sure they will be honest with you.

DON'T PUT IT OFF

You don't need full and complete answers to all four of the questions above before you move forward. Start investigating possibilities for service even as you continue to think through your responses to the questions.

Visit www.missionfinder.org/retirees.html for a comprehensive clearinghouse of opportunities for retirees, both paid and unpaid.

Other helpful websites:
- www.finishers.org (Finishers Project)
- www.rvics.com (Roving Volunteers in Christ's Service)
- www.globalopps.org (Empowering Tentmakers to Reach the World)
- www.christiancareercenter.com/job-seekers/missionary-jobs

UPDATE

In chapter two, we related an experience in which we had struggled back from a camping trip on a Mississippi River island, misled by a map which failed to show the change in a river channel. At that point the issue of what to do with our older years looked all too similar to our camping trip.

We're happy to report that although we aren't completely resolved about everything, God is opening doors and things have gotten better since then. We are more confident now that "we are God's handiwork, created in Christ Jesus to do good works, which God prepared in advance for us to do" (Eph 2:10).

Sandy has been asked to coteach a Sunday school class of fifth and sixth graders, only a shade younger than her favorite age. Contacts with internationals have blossomed. Even though we didn't find the international students we expected to find, there is a large immigrant population here. We now tutor immigrants in English in three different settings each week—an adult education center, the townhouse complex we mentioned in chapter twelve and our own home.

And then there's the Red Sea Cafe.

Only a couple of blocks from the gleaming tall buildings of the Mayo Clinic, the Red Sea Cafe is a different world. It's next door to the mosque where Somali and Sudanese Muslim immigrants pray. We had gone into the café once out of curiosity and found it full of older Somali men conversing in their own language. We felt out of place—Sandy especially, with her head uncovered—and ducked out.

Several months ago Dale decided to go back to the Red Sea Cafe by himself to see if he could strike up a conversation. He did, and he has continued to go almost every week since then. He tries to get there shortly after morning prayers at the mosque, when the café tends to fill up. Dale finds that many of the Muslim men speak some English and are willing to talk with him. Conversations in the café tend to be generalized and take in everybody in the place, so often Dale just sits and drinks spicy Somali tea and listens. Sometimes someone translates the gist of the conversation into English for him.

We're pretty sure Dale is the only non-African and the only non-Muslim who frequents the Red Sea Cafe. The other patrons don't quite know what to do with him. Some are friendly; others are suspicious. One man saw him come in and demanded, "Are *you* here again?" The proprietor spoke up from behind the counter: "He's *always* here."

So among other involvements, Dale is occupied with just being there, building a bridge with Muslim men in an obscure corner of Rochester, Minnesota. He doesn't know where it's going, but he knows, as both of us know, that it's not over yet.

Appendix

Instructions for the Group Leader

You may be using this study guide in several possible settings: an adult Sunday school class, a small-group Bible study in a home, a discussion group in a senior living center or some other situation.

Regardless of the setting, your participants are almost sure to be senior adults. They will come to the study with unique attributes, which you need to take into account. Although this book maintains that "it's not over yet," many seniors assume that it *is* over—not life itself but the productive and creative and influential part of their life span. Inertia, both physical and spiritual, often sets in. Older adults may find themselves growing increasingly cautious about taking on new projects. Vision problems can make them hesitate to drive at night, which limits their involvements. Women who have been diagnosed with osteoporosis—and there are *millions* of them—can develop a fear of falling, which leads to increased caution in general. In a more positive vein, many older adults feel that their lives are already full. They have a longstanding circle of friends and are not looking for new relationships. If their children and grandchildren live nearby, much of their time is taken up with family. They may feel they don't have space in their lives to involve themselves in something new.

On the other hand, older adults can be a joy for a Bible study leader. They usually have a broader knowledge of the Bible than younger participants, and they quote it with closer familiarity, having grown up in a time when the words of Scripture permeated everyday life. They respect the authority of the Bible. They are often more committed to missions, especially denominational missions. As we point out in chapter seven, seniors are not looking to build a resumé. They are less focused on personal advancement and more willing to commit themselves to activities that don't pay. They can control their own schedules. They sometimes have more financial resources than younger people. And they have just plain lived longer, both in the everyday world and in company with Christ. They have piled up years of experiences from which to draw life lessons.

Prepare for each session by completing all five sections of each study on your own prior to meeting with your group. The element of time and the interests of your group will determine how you should approach your meeting. Depending on your group, you may not be able to give full weight to all five sections of each session. Consider these suggestions for how to use the five sections of each session in various kinds of settings:

- **Personal Narrative.** This true story may be read aloud to begin the session, although it is not necessary. You may summarize the Personal Narrative or ask someone in the group to summarize it. The stories presented in this study guide vary widely, and group members will identify with each of them on different levels. The questions at the end of each Personal Narrative are written to help group members find common ground with the person or people in the story. Remember that the story will be new to group members who have not read it in advance, and everyone should be given some time to reflect on it. Encourage group members to discuss their responses to both the Personal Narrative and the questions posed after it. Responses may be spoken or may remain unspoken.
- **Connecting with a Bible Character.** This biblical account in story form sets the stage for the Bible study to follow. You might ask one or more group members to read the account aloud as expressively as possible. Note that while the stories are somewhat fictionalized, they never conflict with the corresponding passage of Scripture. If your time is limited to an hour or so, such as in a Sunday school class, you will probably need

to briefly summarize this section or even skip it and go directly to the Bible Study. If you choose to skip it, suggest that members read it on their own, beforehand if possible.

- **Bible Study.** Ask a group member or members to read the Scripture passage aloud. Group members may or may not have done this section in advance. Allow time for everyone to consider each question and respond. The Bible Study questions help participants understand and apply the Scripture for themselves. Do not assume there is one right answer for every question. Do not be afraid of silence; refrain from jumping in and offering your own answers while people are still thinking. The questions often build on each other, so questions should not be skipped unless you find they have already been answered in previous discussion.
- **Exploring Possibilities.** Allow some time for each group member to work on this section independently. Even if each person has answered the Exploring Possibilities questions in advance, your time together may inspire new thoughts. If it seems appropriate, you may pick out a question or two for group discussion. Your group may begin to formulate plans for a way to serve, something that you can all do together. Perhaps you

have some unfinished plans that were sparked by an earlier session in the book; if so, this could be the place to continue with those plans.
- **Praying into the Future.** Even if your time is limited, allow time for prayer at the end of each session. This prayer time should be more than a routine conclusion to your meeting. During the session you have looked at people from both inside and outside the pages of the Bible who have been empowered by God to make a difference in the world. Encourage your group to pray that God will use them in similar ways or perhaps in creatively different ways. Keep your group focused on the theme of this book, that God still has plans and purposes for each of you.

SUGGESTIONS FOR GROUP STUDY

Here are two possible scenarios for using *Living Your Legacy*. Feel free to adjust these ideas to the needs and interests of your own group.

ADULT SUNDAY SCHOOL CLASS, APPROXIMATELY 50 MINUTES:

- Personal Narrative—10 minutes. Briefly summarize the story. Allow time to consider and respond to the questions. If your class is large, break into small groups for discussion of the questions.
- Connecting with a Bible Character—0-5 minutes. Summarize or even skip if necessary. You may want to suggest that group members read it on their own if you decide to skip it.
- Bible Study—25 minutes. Read the Scripture and go through the questions as a whole group.
- Exploring Possibilities—10 minutes. Allow time for group members to work independently on their responses. You may pick out a question or two for group discussion. Break into small groups for discussion if your class is large. The class may begin to formulate plans for a way to serve together.
- Praying into the Future—5 minutes. Encourage group members to offer *brief* spoken prayers so as many as possible have time to pray aloud. Assure group members that it is not necessary to pray aloud, but all will be

encouraged to hear each other's prayers. If your class is large, break into small groups for prayer. Close the prayer time yourself.

HOME BIBLE STUDY, APPROXIMATELY 90-120 MINUTES:

- Personal Narrative—15-20 minutes. Ask a group member to read the story aloud, or summarize it if you are sure that everyone has read it in advance. Allow time to consider and respond to the questions. You will have more time to expand on answers and respond to each other's answers than you would have in a Sunday school class. Even if your group is small, you may want to break into smaller groups for more in-depth discussion.
- Connecting with a Bible Character—10 minutes. Ask one or more group members to read the account aloud as expressively as possible. If the biblical incident is familiar to most of you, you might briefly discuss how the story has given you a new perspective on a Bible character, but don't let this section take precedence over the Bible Study to come.

- Bible Study—30-40 minutes. Ask a group member or members to read the Scripture passage aloud. Give group members time to respond to each question.
- Exploring Possibilities—20-30 minutes. The more open-ended time frame of a home Bible study allows your group to spend more time working on this section and discussing possibilities for ways you can serve, either as individuals or as a group. Even if your group is small, you may want to break into smaller groups for more detailed discussion, then come back together to share ideas. You may spend several meetings developing specific plans for something you can do together.
- Praying into the Future—15-20 minutes. Here is another place where your more open-ended schedule helps your group. Pray about your individual possibilities for service and about what you might be able to do as a group.

Notes

Chapter 1: Cast Off Security

"By leaving his father's household": John H. Walton, Victor H. Matthews and Mark W. Chavalas, "Abraham Travels to Canaan," in *The IVP Bible Background Commentary: Old Testament* (Downers Grove, Ill.: InterVarsity Press, 2000), p.43.

"Since the northern and central deserts": "Major Trade Routes in the Ancient Near East," in ibid., p.71.

Chapter 2: Engage with the Unexpected

"Two hundred miles on foot": N.T. Wright, *Acts for Everyone, Part 2* (Louisville, Ky.: Westminster John Knox, 2008), p.59.

"The unique phrase *the Spirit of Jesus*": Conrad Gempf, "Acts," in *New Bible Commentary: 21st Century Edition,* ed. D.A. Carson, R.T. France, J.A. Motyer and G.J. Wenham (Downers Grove, Ill.: InterVarsity Press, 1994), p.1089.

"For whatever reason": G.F. Hawthorne, "Holy Spirit," in *Dictionary of the Later New Testament & Its Developments*, ed. Ralph P. Martin and Peter H. Davids (Downers Grove, Ill.: InterVarsity Press, 1997), on *The Essential IVP Reference Collection* CD-ROM (Downers Grove, Ill.: InterVarsity Press, 2003), paragraph 5844.

"Sometimes the Spirit speaks through": Ibid., paragraph 5861.

Chapter 4: Rescue the Helpless

"The medical staff worked": "Milwaukee to Haiti (Update Jan 25, 2010)—Final Blog," *Christian Courier*, www.christiancouriernewspaper.com/blogbase/?m=201001, accessed January 27, 2010.

"It's just amazing, life-changing": "Treating Haitian Kids' Psychological Trauma," Making a Difference segment on *NBC Nightly News*, www.msnbc.msn.com/id/34276015/vp/35068027#35068027, accessed Jan. 26, 2010.

"The origins of the Samaritans": H.G.M. Williamson, "Samaritans," in *Dictionary of Jesus and the Gospels*, ed. Joel B. Green, Scot

McKnight and I. Howard Marshall (Downers Grove, Ill.: InterVarsity Press, 1992), pp.725-26.

"Jews and Samaritans traditionally": Craig S. Keener, *The IVP Bible Background Commentary: New Testament* (Downers Grove, Ill.: InterVarsity Press, 1993), p.218.

In the autumn of 2010: See Lindsey Seavert, "After Flood, Volunteers Save Zumbro Falls Christmas," http://minnesota.cbslocal.com/2010/12/18/zumbro-fallsflood-christmas-disaster-recovery-christmas, accessed Dec. 18, 2010.

Chapter 5: Build Something New

Second Peter 2:5 strongly implies: See W.E. Vine, Merrill F. Unger and William White Jr., "Preacher," in *Vine's Complete Expository Dictionary of Old and New Testament Words* (Nashville: Thomas Nelson, 1996), p.482.

"When all the people around him": Walter C. Kaiser Jr., Peter H. Davids, F.F. Bruce and Manfred T. Brauch, *Hard Sayings of the Bible* (Downers Grove, Ill.: InterVarsity Press, 1996), p.110.

"The ark that Noah builds": "Ark," in *Dictionary of Biblical Imagery,* ed. Leland Ryken, James C. Wilhoit and Tremper Longman III (Downers Grove, Ill.: Inter-Varsity Press, 1998), p.42.

"Noah's ark was not designed": John H. Walton, Victor H. Matthews and Mark W. Chavalas, *The IVP Bible Background Commentary: Old Testament* (Downers Grove, Ill.: InterVarsity Press, 2000), p.37.

Chapter 6: Comfort the Downcast

Two Greek words: See "Comfort, Comforter, Comfortless" in *Vine's Complete Expository Dictionary of Old and New Testament Words* (Nashville: Thomas Nelson, 1996), pp.110-11.

Chapter 7: Empower the Poor

Recently twenty people: Julie Rodakowski, "Boomers Bloom," Rochester, Minn., *Post-Bulletin,* September 18, 2010, p. E4.

"In the Old Testament": John H. Walton, Victor H. Matthews and Mark W. Chavalas, *The IVP Bible Background Commentary: Old Testament*

(Downers Grove, Ill.: InterVarsity Press, 2000), pp.637-38.

Chapter 8: Find an Alternative

"I had ... fallen, like Alice": Michael Gates Gill, *How Starbucks Saved My Life: A Son of Privilege Learns to Live Like Everyone Else* (New York: Gotham Books, 2007), p.174.

Chapter 9: Make a Connection

The agricultural year in Israel: H. Neil Richardson, "Harvest," in *Interpreter's Dictionary of the Bible*, vol. 2., ed. George Arthur Buttrick et al. (Nashville: Abingdon, 1962), p.527.

"Since the bounty of the harvest": John H. Walton, Victor H. Matthews and Mark W. Chavalas, *The IVP Bible Background Commentary: Old Testament* (Downers Grove, Ill.: InterVarsity Press, 2000), p.199.

Chapter 10: Notice the Children Around You

"Son, you are too young.": Information for this chapter came from the following sources: Norman Rohrer, *The Indomitable Mr. O.* (Grand Rapids: Child Evangelism Fellowship Press, 1970); Ruth Overholtzer, *From Then Till Now* (Warrenton, Mo.: Child Evangelism Fellowship Press, 1990); Child Evangelism Fellowship website, www.cefonline.com.

"The common teachability of children": "Child, Children," in *Dictionary of Biblical Imagery*, ed. Leland Ryken, James C. Wilhoit and Tremper Longman III (Downers Grove, Ill.: InterVarsity Press, 1998), p.141.

Chapter 11: Take the Lead

Eliza Davis George: Information for this chapter can be found in Lorry Lutz, *Born to Lose, Bound to Win: The Amazing Journey of Mother Eliza George* (Irvine, Calif.: Harvest House, 1980).

Chapter 12: Welcome the Stranger

At this time in history: Thomas O. Lambdin, "Ethiopia," in *Interpreter's Dictionary of the Bible*, vol. 2., ed. George Arthur Buttrick et al. (Nashville: Abingdon, 1962), p.176.

"From the time of Ptolemy II": Fred D. Gealy, "Ethiopian Eunuch," in ibid., p.178.

"Though taught along with reading aloud": Craig S. Keener, *The IVP Bible Background Commentary: New Testament* (Downers Grove, Ill.: InterVarsity Press, 1993), p.346.

"The pentateuchal laws regarding aliens": R.J.D. Knauth, "Alien, Foreign Resident," in *Dictionary of the Old Testament: Pentateuch*, ed. T. Desmond Alexander and David W. Baker (Downers Grove, Ill.: InterVarsity Press, 2003), p.27.

Chapter 13: Look to the Future

We often see them together: Matthew Stolle, "Franciscan Sister, 88, Continues Her Path," Rochester, Minn., *Post-Bulletin*, May 1, 2010, p. B7.

"To be childless": Craig S. Keener, *The IVP Bible Background Commentary: New Testament* (Downers Grove, Ill.: InterVarsity Press, 1993), p.188.

"According to Luke": Lincoln D. Hurst and Joel B. Green, "Priest, Priesthood," in *Dictionary of Jesus and the Gospels,* ed. Joel B. Green, Scot McKnight and I. Howard Marshall (Downers Grove, Ill.: InterVarsity Press, 1992), pp.634-35.

"Casting incense on the heated altar": Keener, *IVP Bible Background Commentary: NT,* p.189.

Conclusion: What's Next?

We gain a sober judgment: Gordon T. Smith, *Courage and Calling: Embracing Your God-Given Potential* (Downers Grove, Ill.: InterVarsity Press, 1999), p.38.

You may have heard it: Ibid., p.39.

"If I could only be": Ibid., p.42.

"We all see the brokenness": Ibid., pp.42-43, 53.

Carole Perkins is one woman: John Weiss, "When Life Grounds You, Make Coffee,"

Rochester, Minn., *Post-Bulletin*, March 17, 2011, pp. B1, B3.

Back Cover Material

Legacy

Who am I now?

Can I still make a difference?

No matter what stage of life we find ourselves in, we may wonder if what we've done with our time on earth bears any significance. But this question becomes especially important when our expectations for lifelong achievement and ability in later years come face to face with a reality that may not meet those lifelong hopes. It's common to ask, "Who am I now? How should I invest these years? Must I redefine myself, and if so, how? Can I still make a difference?"

Dale and Sandy Larsen found themselves in this place of uncertainty, and they longed to move beyond it into something fruitful and hopeful. Here they offer wisdom born from their experience of finding new, often surprising ways to use their gifts and interests to serve God and those around them. They discovered that even though former roles defined by work and family may be gone or become very different, God still has plans and purposes for their life. And he has plans for your life too.

Join Dale and Sandy in discovering the exciting ways in which God can use you no matter what your age or circumstances may be. rough interaction with personal narratives, Bible studies, prayer, connection points with biblical figures and exercises designed to help you explore new possibilities, you will learn that there's much more to life now than you expected. Rather than just living out your later years, you can learn, with God's help, to live your legacy.

Dale and Sandy Larsen are writers living in Rochester, Minnesota. Together they have written more than thirty books and Bible studies, including the very popular LifeGuide® Bible Study *Growing Older and Wiser*